P9-CFU-649

Dominican Republic

Dominican Republic

BY LURA ROGERS AND
BARBARA RADCLIFFE ROGERS

Enchantment of the World™
Second Series

Children's Press®

An Imprint of Scholastic Inc.

NEW YORK   TORONTO   LONDON   AUCKLAND   SYDNEY
MEXICO CITY   NEW DELHI   HONG KONG
DANBURY, CONNECTICUT

Frontispiece: A Dominican cabin and coconut grove by the sea

Consultant: Richard Abisla, International Observer, Civic Council of Grassroots and
Indigenous Groups of Honduras

Please note: All statistics are as up-to-date as possible at the time of publication.

Book production by Herman Adler

Library of Congress Cataloging-in-Publication Data

Rogers Seavey, Lura.
 Dominican Republic / by Lura Rogers and Barbara Radcliffe Rogers.
   p. cm.—(Enchantment of the world. Second series)
 Includes bibliographical references and index.
 ISBN-13: 978-0-531-12097-2
 ISBN-10: 0-531-12097-X
 1. Dominican Republic—Juvenile literature. I. Radcliffe, Barbara,
 1939– II. Title. III. Series.
 F1934.2.R64 2008
 972.93—dc22   2008000087

SCHOLASTIC, CHILDREN'S PRESS, and associated logos are trademarks and/or registered
trademarks of Scholastic Inc.
1 2 3 4 5 6 7 8 9 10 R 18 17 16 15 14 13 12 11 10 09

Acknowledgments

Many thanks to the staff at Hall Memorial Library in Northfield, New Hampshire. This book is dedicated to the hardworking baseball players of the Dominican Republic, for never forgetting their roots and bringing joy to children and adults everywhere. *Muchas gracias, Papi.*

Cover photo:
Boats at Boca
de Yuma

Contents

Farmland

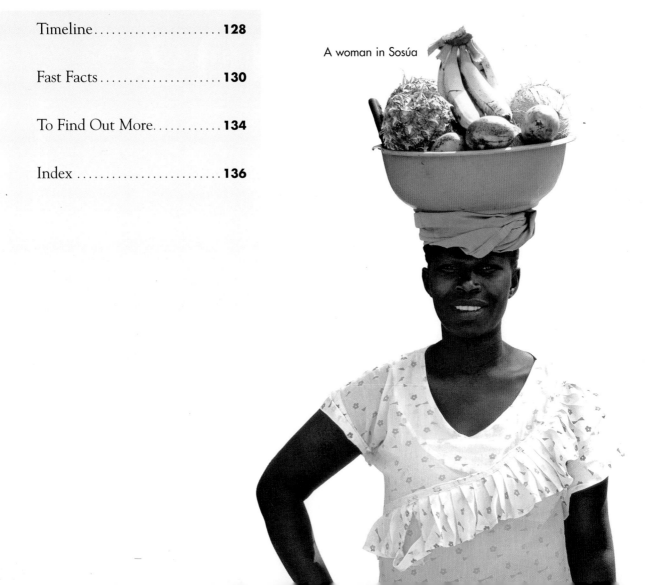

A woman in Sosúa

The Winds of Change

8

This small, palm-fringed beach is in Samaná Bay. Visitors can reach it only on foot or by boat.

Opposite: The Dominican Republic has thousands of miles of beautiful coastlines.

THE DOMINICAN REPUBLIC IS THE GATEWAY TO THE Caribbean, in more ways than one. It is located on the northern edge of the Caribbean Sea, a part of the Atlantic Ocean that lies between North and South America. This region of islands is also called the West Indies. Many ships entering the Caribbean pass by Hispaniola, the large island that the Dominican Republic shares with the nation of Haiti.

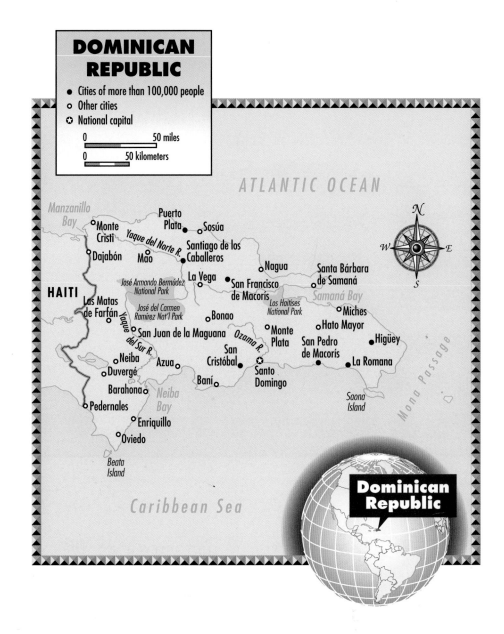

DOMINICAN REPUBLIC

- ● Cities of more than 100,000 people
- ○ Other cities
- ✪ National capital

0   50 miles

0   50 kilometers

ATLANTIC OCEAN

Manzanillo Bay

Monte Cristi

Puerto Plata

Sosúa

Yaque del Norte R.

Santiago de los Caballeros

Dajabón

Mao

Nagua

Santa Bárbara de Samaná

La Vega

HAITI

José Armando Bermúdez National Park

San Francisco de Macorís

Samaná Bay

Las Matas de Farfán

José del Carmen Ramírez Nat'l Park

Los Haitises National Park

Miches

Bonao

Hato Mayor

Yaque del Sur R.

San Juan de la Maguana

Monte Plata

San Pedro de Macorís

Higüey

Ozama R.

Neiba

Azua

San Cristóbal

Santo Domingo

La Romana

Duvergé

Baní

Barahona

Neiba Bay

Mona Passage

Pedernales

Saona Island

Enriquillo

Oviedo

Beata Island

Caribbean Sea

N
W   E
S

Dominican Republic

The Dominican Republic is also the gateway to the Caribbean because learning about it can help you understand its island neighbors. The nation's forested mountains and long, beautiful beaches look much like those of the other islands. The mix of people, the *merengue* music, and the Dominicans' often easygoing attitude represent the island cultures as well.

The modern history of the Americas began in 1492 when explorer Christopher Columbus guided three ships to the island of Hispaniola. There, he would establish the first European colony in the Western Hemisphere. The trade winds—steady

Christopher Columbus and his men landed on the island of Hispaniola in 1492. Taíno and Ciboney people were already living there.

winds that blow over the tropics toward the equator—that filled the sails of his ships could just as well be called the winds of change. Columbus's ships, and later ones that rode the trade winds toward the Caribbean, carried people, plants, animals, and ideas that would change Hispaniola and neighboring islands forever. One early change was tragic: the Taíno people who lived on the island were soon wiped out.

The ships that came after Columbus carried more Spaniards. Some of these Spaniards attacked Taíno villages on Hispaniola.

Not all the changes blown by the trade winds have been bad. Absorbing the best from the peoples who have settled there, the Dominican Republic has taken its place among the nations of the world. It has grown and changed. To these winds it owes the rhythms of its music and many of the customs of its people. Today, travelers still head to the Dominican Republic from all over the world. But unlike early travelers who came to trade and raid, these new visitors stay and play.

A couple dances to merengue music at a beach club in Las Terrenas. The Dominican Republic's rich culture and stunning beaches attract travelers from around the world.

Mountaintops in the Sea

This aerial view shows boats anchored in Bayahibe Harbor on the country's south coast.

The Dominican Republic occupies the eastern two-thirds of the island of Hispaniola. This island and all the others in the West Indies are the peaks of the Greater Antilles mountain chain, the bases of which lie deep beneath the sea. Hispaniola is about 600 miles (950 kilometers) southeast of Miami, Florida. The Atlantic Ocean forms its northern coast, while the warm waters of the Caribbean Sea wash the southern shore. To the east lies the Mona Passage, a rough stretch of water that separates Hispaniola from the island of

Opposite: **Mountains and sea dominate the Dominican landscape.**

What's in a Name?

The West Indies got their name because of a mistake. When the explorer Christopher Columbus arrived in the Caribbean, he was trying to reach a destination on the other side of the world, a part of East Asia called the Indies. The region where he landed soon became known as the West Indies. Columbus named the island where the Dominican Republic is now located La Isla Española, which means "The Spanish Island." Hispaniola is a shortened version of that early name.

The Dominican Republic's Geographic Features

Area: 18,816 square miles (48,734 sq km)

Highest Elevation: Pico Duarte, 10,417 feet (3,175 m)

Lowest Elevation: Lago Enriquillo, 150 feet (46 m) below sea level

Largest Lake: Lago Enriquillo, 25 miles (40 km) long

Longest River: Yaque del Norte, 184 miles (296 km) long

Average Temperatures: July, 81°F (27°C); January, 75°F (24°C)

Average Annual Rainfall: 100 inches (250 cm) in the mountains; 50 inches (130 cm) in the valleys

Greatest Distance East to West: About 240 miles (385 km)

Greatest Distance North to South: About 170 miles (275 km)

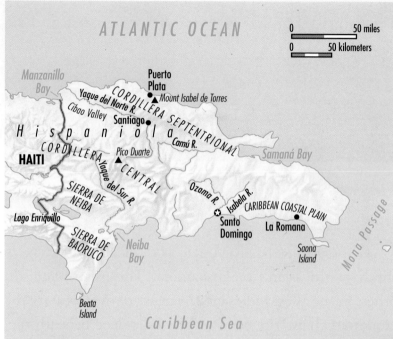

Puerto Rico. The country of Haiti occupies the western third of the island.

The Dominican Republic covers an area of 18,816 square miles (48,734 sq km), which is almost the size of the states of New Hampshire and Vermont combined. Miles of white sandy beaches line its coasts, and chains of rugged mountains rise inland. Rivers flowing down the mountains create fertile valleys, which are ideal for farming.

A Peek at the Mountains

Mountains cover about 80 percent of the Dominican Republic. Four major mountain ranges spread across the country. The largest of these is the Cordillera Central, which includes Pico Duarte (Duarte Peak), the highest point in the West Indies. At 10,417 feet (3,175 meters), Pico Duarte is sometimes covered with a layer of frost that makes it look snowcapped. The Cordillera Central is the backbone of the central region. To the north, the Cordillera Septentrional rises from the plains along the Atlantic coast. In contrast to the grand mountains of the central range, its highest peaks reach only about 3,000 feet (1,000 m). In the southwest, the Sierra de Neiba and the Sierra de Baoruco overlook a lake-filled valley.

Pico Duarte is the highest peak in the West Indies. It is part of Armando Bermúdez National Park.

The Yaque del Norte winds around the hills in Cordillera Central.

Water from the Mountains

Most of the Dominican Republic's major rivers spring from the mountains of the Cordillera Central. The Yaque del Norte River begins at an elevation of 8,462 feet (2,579 m), near Pico Duarte. Its waters travel for 184 miles (296 km) until reaching the sea at Monte Cristi on the northwest coast.

The Yaque del Sur flows down the southern side of Pico Duarte. For about three-quarters of its length, it runs through the mountains, finally reaching Neiba Bay on the southern coast. The Isabela and the Ozama rivers begin in the lower regions east of the Cordillera Central and meet the sea at Santo Domingo, the nation's capital and largest city.

Juan Pablo Duarte

Pico Duarte, the highest point in the West Indies, was named for Juan Pablo Duarte (right), a leader of the independence movement that freed the Dominican Republic from the rule of Haiti. Duarte was born into a wealthy family and spent seven years studying overseas. When he returned in 1833, he was determined to free his people from Haiti's tyranny. In 1838, Duarte and a group of like-minded Dominicans formed a secret society called *La Trinitaria*. The members of this group opposed the harsh rule of Haitian dictator Jean-Pierre Boyer and spent years plotting to overthrow him. Finally, Duarte's followers captured the capital city of Santo Domingo. They declared independence for the Dominican Republic on February 27, 1844.

Below the Slopes

The Cibao Valley lies below the southern slopes of the Cordillera Septentrional. This fertile region covers about 150 square miles (400 sq km). The Yaque del Norte helps make the land fertile. After heavy rainfalls, soil washes down from the mountains into the river. The river deposits this nutrient-filled soil in the Cibao Valley. Water from the river also irrigates the valley's cropland. The rich soil of this region makes it a major center for growing tobacco and grains. The city of Santiago sits at the eastern end of the Cibao Valley.

Fertile soil and water from the Yaque del Norte help produce abundant rice crops in the Cibao Valley.

The Amber Coast

The northern coast of the Dominican Republic is known as the Amber Coast because the hills there contain a rich supply of amber. Amber is a form of tree resin, a soft substance found inside trees. When trapped underground or underwater for millions of years, the resin turns to fossil and becomes hard. The yellowish amber perfectly preserves insects (right), flowers, and objects that became trapped in its sticky resin millions of years ago. Craftspeople and artists often shape and polish amber to make jewelry.

In the southwest, a narrow passage of water, called a strait, once separated two mountain ranges that now enclose the Neiba Valley. Shifting lands trapped a pocket of saltwater to form Lago Enriquillo (Lake Enriquillo), the largest lake on Hispaniola. Larger than the island of Manhattan, Lago Enriquillo stretches for 25 miles (40 km). At 150 feet (46 m) below sea level, it is the lowest point in the West Indies. It is home to varied wildlife, including crocodiles. The area surrounding the lake has a hot, dry climate.

A coastal plain spreads along the southern coast. Sugarcane plantations fill this low, flat region. It is also the site of Santo Domingo.

When It Rains, It Pours

The Dominican Republic has a hot, tropical climate. Average temperatures range from 75 degrees Fahrenheit (24 degrees Celsius) in January to 81°F (27°C) in July. Winds off the sea help relieve the coastal heat. Along the coast and in protected valleys, temperatures can reach 100°F (38°C). Temperatures in the mountains, meanwhile, sometimes drop to 32°F (0°C).

Rainy and dry seasons divide the year. During the rainy season, which lasts from May to November, storms come and go quickly, drenching the land and cooling the air. The mountain regions get, on average, 100 inches (250 centimeters) of rain in a year, while the Neiba Valley sees only half that much. The average rainfall for the plains is 60 inches (150 cm).

Children wade down a flooded street in San Cristóbal after a tropical storm hit in 2007.

Storms are common, but hurricanes pose the biggest threat. On average, a serious hurricane hits the island of Hispaniola once every two years. Hurricanes blow off roofs, shatter windows, and even upturn houses. Wind, heavy surf, and flooding uproot trees and destroy crops. In 1930, a devastating hurricane battered the Dominican Republic with winds of 200 miles (325 km) per hour. In 1979, Hurricane David killed two thousand people during its three-day rampage.

In September 1998, Hurricane Georges pounded the Dominican Republic with wind and torrents of rain that washed away whole mountainsides. The storm left more than five hundred people dead or missing, five hundred more seriously injured, nearly three hundred thousand homeless, and 80 percent of the nation's crops and livestock destroyed. Repairing the storm damage cost an estimated US$6 billion.

Hurricane Georges slammed the Dominican Republic in 1998. Hundreds of people were killed and thousands lost their homes.

Looking at Dominican Cities

Santo Domingo, the capital of the Dominican Republic, is the nation's largest city. The second largest, with a population of 690,548, is Santiago de los Caballeros (right), which people call simply Santiago. Founded in 1494, Santiago lies on the Yaque del Norte River in the northwest part of the country. An earthquake destroyed Santiago in 1564, but people rebuilt it. Today, the city is at the heart of the Dominican Republic's tobacco-growing region. Important sites in the city include the Monument to the Heroes of the Restoration and the Cathedral of Santiago.

Beautiful beaches and a colonial fort called San Felipe make the northern coastal town of Puerto Plata (left), which has a population of 255,061, central to the Dominican tourism industry. The town sits near Mount Isabel de Torres, which rises to 2,600 feet (800 m). A cable car carries visitors to the top for a view over the city and the Atlantic Ocean.

La Romana, east of Santo Domingo on the southern coast, has a population of 191,303. The history of La Romana is closely intertwined with the Gulf and Western company. Until the 1980s, the company owned nearly the entire town. Company officials managed the company's sugar-growing, sugar-refining, cattle-raising, and cement businesses from La Romana. After loud public criticism of its operations, the company spent millions of dollars to improve local schools, hospitals, and housing—and its own reputation. Today, La Romana is renowned for Altos de Chavón, a modern village in a variety of historic styles.

Natural Neighbors

THE DOMINICAN REPUBLIC IS A SMALL COUNTRY, BUT IT contains a wide variety of plant and animal life. Habitats range from beaches and mountaintops to deserts and rain forests. Each of these zones has its own kinds of trees, plants, birds, and animals.

Opposite: **Caribbean king palms rise from the grassland in the southern Dominican Republic.**

Plant Life

The types of plants that grow in the Dominican Republic change with variations in the country's elevation and climate.

A variety of plants cover the mountains in the Dominican Republic.

A Hispaniolan pine tree grows near the summit of Pico Duarte.

Mountain peaks, some reaching elevations of more than 10,000 feet (3,000 m), are often covered with coniferous (cone-bearing) trees such as the Hispaniolan pine. The *Reserva Científica Valle Nuevo* (New Valley Scientific Reserve) protects stands of untouched forest so no one cuts them down.

A warmer climate allows lush rain forests to cover the lower mountainsides. Trees such as mahogany and satinwood grow in the rain forest. People cut these trees for their valuable wood. Mahogany from the eastern mountains was used to build the first cathedral for the European conquerors. The rain forests are also home to cedar, juniper, and lignum vitae. Food-bearing plants such as star apple, wild guava, wild pepper, calabash, cashew, and soursop flourish in the rain forest.

Vegetation in the Dominican rain forests can be varied and lush.

Along the beaches, royal palms spread their leaves over the hot sand, shading beachgoers. These trees are native to the Dominican Republic. The coconut palm, which people imported from Africa, also grows along the shore. Cactus and agave plants grow in the dry areas near Lago Enriquillo and on the plains. In areas with a more moderate climate, Dominican magnolia grows along with the ceiba (silk-cotton tree), which can live for three hundred years.

Before the Europeans arrived, the Taíno people raised crops that were native to the island. They used the calabash tree for food and dried its gourds to make masks and containers. The cassava plant was their main food, and they also grew papaya, pepper, and tobacco. Europeans first encountered tobacco when they arrived on the island of Hispaniola.

Agave plants bloom in an arid region of the Dominican Republic. Agave is one of thousands of plant species in the country.

Farms Versus Forests

Deforestation—the loss of forests—is a serious problem in the Dominican Republic. Slash-and-burn farming, which the government has banned since the 1970s, causes a major portion of the damage.

The practice of slash-and-burn farming involves burning the trees and brush to make new farmland. At first, the soil is fertile and crops grow well. But without the sturdy root system of the forest to hold the good topsoil in place, rainwater easily washes it off the sloping fields. Farmers cannot grow crops in the poor soil beneath, so they abandon the land, burn a new plot, and repeat the cycle.

Besides destroying habitat for animals, deforestation leaves the nation more vulnerable to mudslides during heavy rains. Mud flowing down the mountainside can destroy houses.

The Dominican Republic has had some success in ending deforestation. In 1973, an estimated 16 percent of the Dominican Republic was forested. Today, some forests have been replanted, and about 25 percent of the island is wooded.

People have found more than 5,600 species of plants in the Dominican Republic. But only about 35 percent of these grew on Hispaniola before the first Europeans arrived. Europeans introduced the country's biggest cash crop—sugarcane. They also brought other products now common in the Caribbean, including coffee, bananas, and mangoes. Citrus fruits and cocoa came from Central and South America. As traders traveled around the world, they brought Australian eucalyptus, Indian almond trees, and Pacific Island breadfruit trees.

Most animals that live in the Dominican Republic are native to the island, but Europeans also brought animals that were new to Hispaniola. The Spanish brought cows and pigs as livestock and donkeys and horses for doing work. Rats and mice came as unwanted stowaways on ships, so Europeans brought cats and mongooses to help control them. These animals upset the balance of the island's ecology so much that many native species have been lost entirely or are seriously endangered.

The solenodon is a rare rodent native to Haiti and the Dominican Republic. Its biggest threats are predators such as cats, dogs, and mongooses, and the loss of its forest habitat.

Among the native species that remain are many kinds of reptiles, rodents, and insects. The rhinoceros iguana and the ricard iguana, both endangered species, inhabit the warmer regions. Snakes, lizards, and noisy little frogs can be found all over. Crocodiles and variegated-shell turtles live in the salty waters of Lago Enriquillo. Both alligators and crocodiles are found in other Dominican waters. The solenodon, a small rodent that resembles an anteater, feeds on a variety of insects. It is nearly extinct now, along with its rodent relative the jutía. The agouti, a pest that destroys sugarcane crops, is one of the few rodents on Hispaniola that the mongoose does not hunt.

Rhinoceros iguanas grow 2 to 4 feet (60 to 120 cm) long. They are endangered in the Dominican Republic.

Friend or Foe?

The mongoose is a small mammal that grows to a length of about 16 inches (41 cm). Its stiff, yellow-tan coat has brown and black hairs mixed in. This feisty little animal is not native to Hispaniola. Early European settlers imported the mongoose to control rodent pests. The mongoose is quick, agile, and fierce tempered. It kills rats and snakes with ease. It also feeds on birds, eggs, and other small animals. Though mongooses were brought in to control pests, they became the worst pests of all. The mongooses multiplied quickly and destroyed a large percentage of the native bird population on Hispaniola.

Making Pigs of Themselves

No one knows exactly what became of the eight pigs that Christopher Columbus brought to Hispaniola in 1493. But historians do know that twenty-four pigs brought to the neighboring island of Cuba in 1498 multiplied to thirty thousand by the year 1514. The two islands have similar climates and vegetation, so it is reasonable to guess that by 1509 the Spanish colonists of Hispaniola were overrun by as many as ten thousand pigs.

Sea Life

The warm waters off the Dominican Republic teem with fish and other aquatic life.

The warm waters off the Caribbean and Atlantic coasts abound with life. Crabs and snails live along the beaches and in tidal pools, while the sea is full of fish. Some are smaller than your

little finger; others weigh as much as 500 pounds (225 kilograms). Turtles, barracudas, eels, parrotfish, and sawfish cruise the coastal waters. Shrimps, mullets, red snappers, sardines, mackerels, and oysters all find their way from the Caribbean onto Dominican dinner plates.

Miles of coral reefs line the undersea coasts. Skeletons of tiny creatures called coral polyps form the reefs. Living corals are colorful and often have soft, flexible shapes. Fish and other sea creatures make their homes among the coral reefs, which protect smaller fish from deep-sea predators. The reefs are very fragile. Changes in water temperature or the chemicals and nutrients found in water can easily damage them. Pollution now threatens the Dominican reefs.

Coral reefs are one of the Dominican Republic's most beautiful and precious natural assets.

From December through March, herds of humpback whales visit the Dominican coast off Samaná Bay. The region is also home to bottlenose dolphins and Caribbean manatees. Although fishing and pollution have depleted much of the coastal wildlife, less-developed areas are still rich with life.

A Cow That Swims?

The manatee, which is sometimes called a sea cow, is a large mammal that lives in the coastal waters of the Caribbean. This mild-tempered animal is a vegetarian. It eats up to 100 pounds (45 kg) of water plants a day, using its upper lip like pliers to bite. The manatee has gray skin and bristly hairs, with front "legs" shaped like paddles. Its tail is rounded, and it has no rear limbs. Caribbean manatees sometimes reach 13 feet (4 m) long and can weigh 3,500 pounds (1,600 kg). Hunting has made this gentle animal species endangered.

The National Bird

The Dominican national bird is the palmchat, which lives only on Hispaniola and nearby tiny islands. Palmchats are small and slender but very loud. They tend to stay in groups, and their chirps make a clamor. Palmchats also nest together. As many as thirty pairs of palmchats use sticks to build large group nests. These nests are usually high in royal palm trees.

Bird Life

About two thousand species of birds live in the Dominican Republic. Pink flamingos stand out against the bright blue waters of the coast. Spoonbills, ibis, herons, ducks, and pelicans also live near water. Forests are home to many types of colorful parrots, including the rare Hispaniolan parrot. Nightingales sing alongside more common swallows and pigeons. Los Haitises National Park, on Samaná Bay, is a bird sanctuary and historical site. The reserve protects rare birds and extensive cave systems that hold inscriptions made by Taínos long ago.

A flock of pink flamingos wades into the water at Barahona in the southwest.

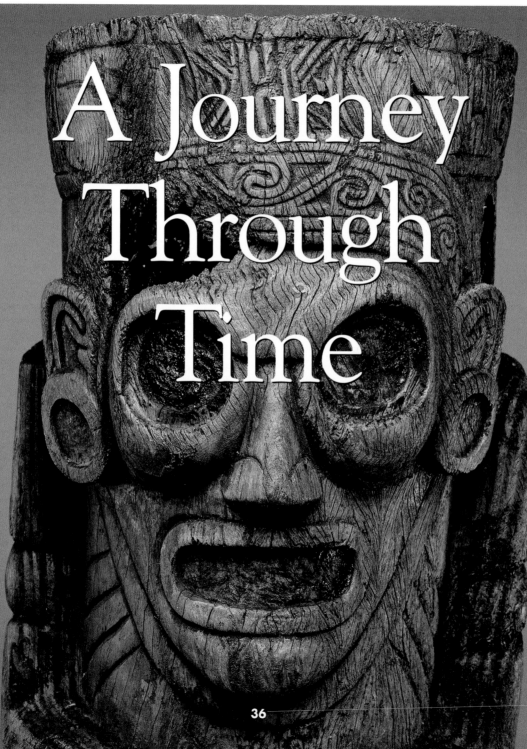

A Journey Through Time

PEOPLE HAD BEEN LIVING ON HISPANIOLA FOR THOUSANDS of years by the time Christopher Columbus set foot there. The first people to settle on the island arrived from South America between 4000 and 3000 B.C. More than three thousand years later, in about A.D. 300, a group of Arawak people from the Orinoco Valley, in what is now the South American nation of Venezuela, traveled to the island. They formed a settlement on the eastern tip and named the island Quisqueya. More Arawaks arrived in the following centuries, gradually mixing with the original inhabitants, who had by then become farmers. Calling themselves the Taíno, meaning "good" or "noble," the farming people distinguished themselves from the more aggressive, roaming Arawaks, also called Caribs.

Opposite: **A Taíno carved this wooden vessel, most likely before Christopher Columbus arrived in the Americas. People have lived in what is now the Dominican Republic for thousands of years.**

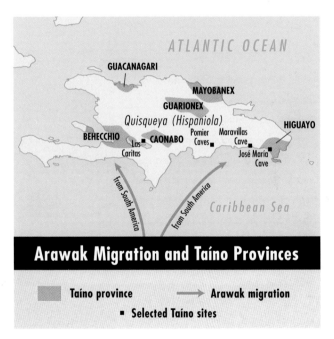

Arawak Migration and Taíno Provinces

Taíno province   Arawak migration
■ Selected Taíno sites

Taínos grew corn, sweet potatoes, beans, squash, and cassava for food. They also cultivated cotton, tobacco, and the calabash—a large gourd they used as a container for food and water. They developed agricultural techniques to help their crops grow. They learned to heap mounds of soil into rows as beds for the seedlings.

Taínos made long canoes from ceiba trees. These canoes held as many as 150 people. Taínos also built simple wooden houses with thatched (straw) roofs.

Taíno society was organized into villages housing one thousand to two thousand people. A chief called a *cacique*, who could be either male or female, ruled each village. Villages were grouped into regional provinces, each with its own leader. By the time Europeans landed on the island, between five hundred thousand and one million Taínos were living on the island in a peaceful, well-organized culture.

Ancient Art

The Taíno people often drew or carved pictures in the caves of Hispaniola. Pomier Caves, near San Cristóbal in the south, contain some six thousand charcoal drawings made about two thousand years ago. Nowhere in the Caribbean is there a larger collection of art made before the arrival of Columbus. The images depict humans, birds, fish, and other figures.

Several of the caves are on protected land, but not all of them. In the early 2000s, companies mining for limestone destroyed several of the caves. In the years since, the government and private groups have worked to prevent further damage to the caves.

Taíno Beliefs

Taínos believed in many different gods and goddesses. The supreme being was Atabey, the goddess of freshwater and fertility. Her son was Yacahú, the lord of the cassava tree and the sea. Lesser gods and goddesses called *zemis* lived all around them. Taínos carried small carvings of these lesser gods because they believed this would help protect them. The Taíno people also believed that ancestral spirits lived with them in the natural world.

Europeans Arrive

In 1492, the Italian explorer Christopher Columbus, leading a Spanish expedition, visited the island of Hispaniola. He soon sailed back to Spain to tell of his discovery. When he returned to Hispaniola the following year, he landed on the northern coast of the island and founded the town of Isabela, the island's first permanent European settlement. Isabela served as Spain's Caribbean base port until 1496, when Columbus's brother Bartholomew discovered a protected harbor on the southern coast. Here grew the capital city of Santo Domingo, which became the new Spanish political center and base for exploration. The colony as a whole was also called Santo Domingo.

Hispaniola appealed to Columbus for many reasons. It was well located, and it had gold. It also had a large number of Taínos, whom the Spanish soon began exploiting. The Spanish established a system called *encomienda*,

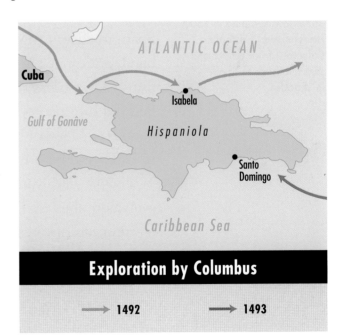

Exploration by Columbus

→ 1492   → 1493

Military leader Francisco de Bobadilla came from Spain to Hispaniola in 1500. He removed Christopher Columbus from power and sent him back to Spain in shackles.

which distributed the land and its native inhabitants among the new Spanish settlers to be used as they wished. In other words, the Taíno became a nation of enslaved people. A small rebellion erupted in 1495 but was quickly stamped out.

The new settlers couldn't get along with one another, and by 1500, Hispaniola was in a civil war. When Spanish military leader Francisco de Bobadilla arrived, he found such chaos that he arrested the Columbus brothers and sent them back to Spain to answer to the queen. He restored order with a heavy hand, and under his harsh rule royal mines were established using slave labor. Ironically, the gold he forced others to find did him no good—a ship carrying de Bobadilla and 600 pounds (270 kg) of gold was wrecked on its way back to Spain in 1502, and both he and the gold were lost.

Nicolás de Ovando, who ruled from 1502 until 1509, was even more abusive. The physical abuse combined with outbreaks of European diseases were too much for the Taíno people. By 1503, the Spaniards were bringing enslaved Africans to replace the Taínos, who had died of illness, malnutrition, overwork, or even suicide. By 1524, just thirty-two years after Columbus's arrival, the Taíno people were essentially gone forever.

A Third Columbus Arrives

At the end of de Ovando's rule, Christopher Columbus's son Diego was sent to govern the colony. Diego was an active leader, responsible for the construction of the Alcázar, the first European fortress in the Americas. He also ordered the construction of its first university, which opened in 1538. Enslaved Africans built both the fort and the university, as well as the quickly rising city of Santo Domingo. Meanwhile, the Spanish had nearly given up on the western end of the island, leaving it in the hands of the new landowners without much, if any, rule.

The Alcázar was built as a palace for Diego Columbus. It dates to about 1517.

Spanish officials were nervous that Diego Columbus might seize too much power, so they established an *audiencia* (council) on the island in 1512. The group watched over the governor and could review and control his policies. By the time Columbus's rule ended in 1526, the council had taken over most of his powers. The audiencia remained in control for many years to come.

As Spain's attention began to turn toward its colonies on the mainland of South and Central America, pirates saw an opportunity to exploit Hispaniola. In 1586, British explorer and pirate Sir Francis Drake seized Santo Domingo and demanded a ransom from the Spanish government for its return. In the 1600s and 1700s, many pirates, including Blackbeard, made the island their stomping ground, and it became headquarters for some. The island appealed to pirates because it had many harbors where ships could hide. The government was poorly organized, so illegal trade was common and smugglers made a good living there.

Sir Francis Drake of England captured Santo Domingo in 1586.

An Island Adrift

Gradually, Spain was losing its grip on Hispaniola. French troops occupied the western end of the island, and they fought with the Spanish for control of the rest. Although the Treaty of Ryswick ended Spain's war with France in 1697 and returned the two armies to opposite ends of Hispaniola, Spain did not give up its claim on the French-occupied land. It was not until eighty years later, with the Treaty of Aranjuez, that Spain finally recognized the French claim to the western part of the island. A formal border was established between the two colonies, and the French section was named Saint-Domingue.

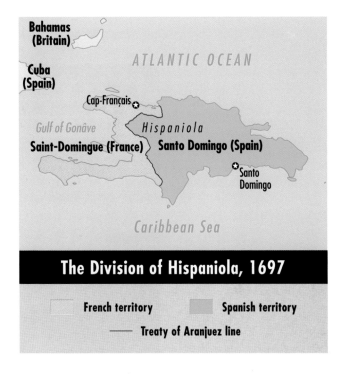

The Division of Hispaniola, 1697

French territory   Spanish territory

—— Treaty of Aranjuez line

Toussaint Louverture led the Haitian independence movement.

Between 1761 and 1810, more than six thousand enslaved people were brought from Africa. During this time, an antislavery revolution brewed in Saint-Domingue. In the 1790s, Toussaint Louverture led a rebellion of enslaved workers. They succeeded in taking over the entire island. Toussaint Louverture was now in charge. Although he had been a slave himself, with the power given to him under the country's new constitution, he created a system of large plantations that were as brutal as those he had opposed.

A Journey Through Time   **43**

Louverture and his men battle French troops. They won the conflict, and Haiti became independent in 1804.

Napoléon I, the leader of France, had been successful in several battles in Europe and wanted to land in North America. To do so, he needed a strong base in the Caribbean to control sea access to southern ports. In 1802, Napoléon sent an army to retake Hispaniola. He expected little resistance, but he was mistaken. Though Toussaint Louverture was captured, his army fought fiercely. In 1803, they defeated the French, and the following year, Haiti was declared an independent nation.

In 1822, Haitian president Jean-Pierre Boyer sent troops into the Spanish part of the island. Haiti now ruled the entire island. In the coming years, the economy and people of Spanish Haiti suffered neglect, and schools and the university closed.

Independence and Strife

In 1838, Juan Pablo Duarte, the son of a wealthy Dominican family, established La Trinitaria, a secret society designed to overthrow Haitian rule and gain independence. On February 27, 1844, Ramón Matías Mella, a supporter of La Trinitaria, led revolutionaries who seized Santo Domingo. The revolutionaries declared independence, and the Dominican Republic was born.

Pedro Santana, another leader in the revolution, became the republic's first president. In 1848, he resigned to take charge of the military. He wanted to prevent another Haitian takeover. Buenaventura Báez now became president, and the two men competed for control. By 1861, the presidency had changed hands between them so often that the nation was torn apart by political unrest. Santana worried about the future of the Dominican Republic, and he asked Queen Isabela II of Spain for help. He thought that if Spain made the Dominican Republic a colony, opposing Haiti would be easier.

Spanish troops arrived, but this "help" didn't work as well as Santana had hoped. Spain imposed new taxes and ruled harshly. Armies of rebels soon rose up. In 1865, the rebels forced the Spanish to withdraw.

Spain regained control of its former colony in 1861, but the Dominicans soon rebelled. Here, Spanish troops battle Dominicans in 1864.

Over the next seventeen years, the presidency changed hands twelve times, and various regions of the country fought among themselves. In 1882, Ulises Heureaux was named president. Although Heureaux ruled as a tyrant, he managed to improve communications by building some railways and installing a telegraph system. Unfortunately, these projects were financed by international loans, and the nation was soon in serious debt. In 1899, Heureaux was assassinated. The next two decades saw continued chaos and constant battling for power.

U.S. Involvement

Foreign governments pressured the Dominican Republic to repay its heavy debt. Meanwhile, the United States solidified its control in the Caribbean. The United States had acquired Caribbean territories after it defeated Spain in the Spanish-American War in 1898. It was not willing to tolerate any instability in the region that would lead to European intervention. Moreover, U.S. president Theodore Roosevelt was building a canal across Panama, the narrowest part of Central America. Because boats would no longer have to travel all the way around the

Ulises Heureaux served as president of the Dominican Republic from 1882 until his death in 1899.

southern tip of South America, the canal would drastically cut the time it took to ship goods from the Atlantic Ocean to the Pacific. Roosevelt didn't want any unrest near the canal, so he intervened in the Dominican Republic.

In 1905, Dominican president Carlos Morales agreed to allow U.S. troops to take over the operation of customs houses, where goods arriving in the Dominican Republic were taxed. The United States took over repayment of the nation's debts while withholding 55 percent of its customs taxes. Even the remaining 45 percent far exceeded the amount the Dominican government had been able to collect before.

Although the nation's financial situation improved, the political situation did not. Rebellions broke out, officials were assassinated, and government leaders were ousted. In 1916, the United States sent in troops. They would occupy the Dominican Republic for eight years. Dominicans were jailed and even killed for criticizing the policies of the occupation.

Workers cut a channel during a failed attempt to build the Panama Canal in the 1880s. In the early 1900s, a second attempt was made, and the canal opened in 1914.

U.S. Marines enter Santo Domingo during the occupation of 1916. American forces remained in the Dominican Republic until 1924.

During the occupation, the Dominican Republic's budget was balanced, and revenues from sugar and other exports increased. Schools and hospitals were built and staffs were trained. Previously, each political party had its own army, but during the U.S. occupation, a national guard was established.

Still, many Dominicans hated the occupation. They were offended by the way U.S. forces treated Dominicans, and they loathed the censorship imposed by U.S. officials. Most of all, they resented having foreigners run their country. The occupation was not popular in the United States either, and by 1924, the U.S. troops were gone.

That same year, President Horacio Vásquez was elected in free elections. The economy began improving, and Santo Domingo was modernized. Meanwhile, a young man named

Rafael Leónidas Trujillo Molina was working his way up through the ranks of the military. By 1930, he was commander of the national army.

The Trujillo Years

In February 1930, Rafael Trujillo became president through rigged elections. He remained in control of the country until 1961. Trujillo's appetite for power and wealth led to many questionable actions. Many of his opponents were arrested or killed.

Rafael Trujillo entered the Dominican army in 1918. By 1927, he was a brigadier general and commander of the army.

In September 1930, during Trujillo's first year in office, a devastating hurricane—one of the worst in Dominican history—served to boost his image. The hurricane gave Trujillo a chance to rebuild the capital city and play the part of a heroic figure in the wake of disaster. At the time, most people thought of him as an ideal leader. But behind the scenes, Trujillo was gaining more and more power. He took control of the congress and other government branches, as well as many large private organizations.

Trujillo succeeded in making the economy stable and finally paid off all foreign debt. Dominican industry expanded, with new roads, railways, airports, and seaports. Farming techniques improved and livestock production increased dramatically, while the mining industry saw its best success in years. A middle class began to emerge for the first time, and more people received education. Trujillo's efforts to raise living standards and provide the poor with government aid improved the lives of many Dominicans. Statistically, this was a golden era. But there was a darker side.

Trujillo ran a tight and brutal dictatorship. His faithful army stifled any serious threats to his career. Opponents disappeared or were murdered. From time to time, Trujillo allowed elections,

A Family Fortune

Trujillo's family built up a fortune based on sugar, land, and anything Trujillo desired. He forced farmers with small plots off their land and built plantations for his family members at government expense. By the end of his rule, his family controlled more than 60 percent of the nation's agriculture and industry. In effect, they owned the country, including twelve of its fifteen sugar mills.

but he always made sure he had no real competition. From 1938 to 1942, his brother Héctor and other trusted associates served as president. But they were puppets. Rafael Trujillo continued to hold all of the true power.

Rafael Trujillo (center) dominated the Dominican Republic for three decades. He served as both the head of the military and the president.

The ruthless Trujillo was assassinated by army leaders in 1961.

As the economy of the Dominican Republic improved, increasing numbers of Haitians began to cross the border to work on Dominican sugar plantations. Trujillo wanted to gain firm control of the border, so, in 1937, he ordered the massacre of Haitians living in the Dominican Republic. Nearly twenty thousand were killed. With the help of bribes, Trujillo was able to cover up the massacre.

In 1960, when Trujillo tried to have the president of Venezuela assassinated because he had criticized Trujillo's dictatorship, the world began to realize what was happening in the Dominican Republic. The Organization of American States (OAS), an organization of all the nations in the Americas, banned the Dominican Republic from membership. The United States broke off relations with the Dominican Republic. The Catholic Church denounced Trujillo. On May 30, 1961, Rafael Trujillo was ambushed and killed. Some people suggested that the United States had supplied the weapons for the attack.

The Struggle Continues

At the time of Trujillo's assassination, the president of the Dominican Republic was Joaquín Balaguer Ricardo. He had been one of Trujillo's puppets, but following Trujillo's murder, he quickly renounced the former dictator and began to relax many of his strict policies. Balaguer successfully prevented the Trujillo family from regaining power and finally forced them out of the country. Despite these changes, Balaguer was ousted in January 1962.

December 20, 1962, was the day of the first free election in the Dominican Republic since 1924. Juan Bosch Gaviño of the Dominican Revolutionary Party (PRD) won. He helped draw up the Constitution of 1963, which separated church and state, gave civilians control over the military, and restored many civil rights. As a result of these changes, the OAS lifted its ban.

The power struggle had not ended, however, and by the end of 1963, the military had overthrown the new president. The country remained a military state until 1965, when the PRD and loyal military officers organized a rebellion. Once again, the

Juan Bosch Gaviño shakes hands with supporters before the presidential election of 1962, which put him into office.

United States moved to protect its interests. President Lyndon Johnson sent in twenty thousand U.S. troops to support the Dominican government in ending the civil war.

The United States now had more to worry about than the island's political instability. The unrest was causing a significant economic impact. After Trujillo's death, U.S. companies had invested more than US$87 million in real estate in the Dominican Republic. They were not going to let a new dictator or government interfere with their plans. The OAS sent in peacekeepers, soldiers charged with preventing conflict, and, in 1966, Balaguer was elected president.

Under this foreign-supervised government, Balaguer made many reforms. During three terms in office, he often appointed members of the opposing political party to government positions, something new in his country. He also restricted military power and prevented the army from interfering in government. Businesses became more profitable, and the government began to help rural people, many of whom lived in poverty. But, like Trujillo, Balaguer used the national police to deal with anyone who opposed him.

American soldiers move through Santo Domingo. In 1965, U.S. president Lyndon Johnson sent U.S. troops to the Dominican Republic to help protect U.S. interests and keep the peace.

Leonel Fernández Reyna (waving) was elected president of the Dominican Republic in 1996 and again in 2004.

Modern Times

By 1978, Dominicans had become dissatisfied with Balaguer. The growing economy had done little to help average Dominicans, and prices were rising quickly. Balaguer lost the presidential election. By 1986, however, he was back in power. He remained president for another ten years, until he was eighty-seven years old.

The progressive leader Leonel Fernández Reyna won the 1996 election. During his time in office, Fernández worked with the United States and other countries to increase trade. He wanted the Dominican Republic to be part of the global economy. In the 2000 elections, PRD candidate Hipólito Mejía was elected. Unfortunately, Mejía's management of finances was poor, and the country's economy went into a tailspin. In 2004, Dominican citizens returned Fernández to office. He managed to stabilize the economy, and by 2007, the nation's economy was again growing.

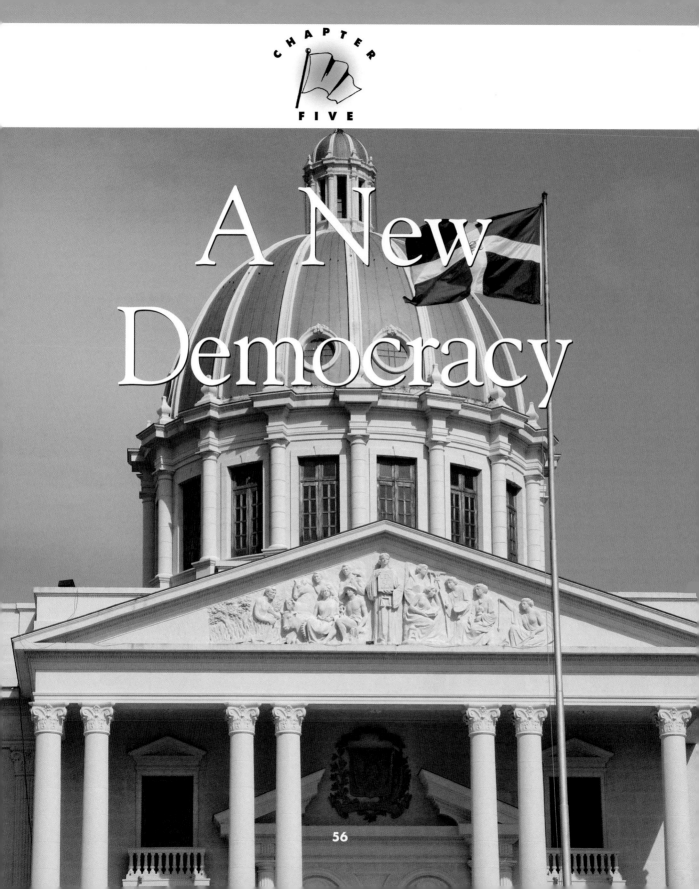

A New Democracy

A FTER YEARS OF DICTATORSHIP AND TURMOIL, THE Dominican Republic is now a multiparty republic. Although Dominicans elect many public officials, they would like still more control of their government. Many do not trust most government officials. Many feel that those in power got there because of their social, political, or business connections, rather than because they are the best people for the job.

Opposite: **After many years of dictatorship, the Dominican Republic is now a democracy.**

Dominicans wait in line to cast ballots in a 2006 election.

The Constitution

The Dominican Republic has had several constitutions, each reflecting the political mood of the time—or, at least, the thinking of the president at the time. The most recent constitution, adopted in 1966, has been amended, or changed, several times. Although the constitution puts few limits on the president's powers, it stresses civil rights and gives citizens liberties they never had been guaranteed before.

In 1978, amendments to the constitution reduced the military's political involvement and prevented the military from ousting a president. These changes also gave the military more civic duties. The armed forces are now responsible for building roads, housing, and medical and educational facilities. They also replant forests and serve as staff at hospitals and schools.

The Dominican Constitution limits the political power of the military. Here, members of the military march in an Independence Day parade in Santo Domingo.

The majestic National Palace in Santo Domingo is the seat of the Dominican government.

The Executive Branch

The Dominican government is divided into three branches: executive, legislative, and judicial. The head of the executive branch is the president, who is elected to a four-year term. A fifteen-member cabinet of ministers assists the president. The Dominican Constitution allows the president broad authority to appoint members of government, including governors, cabinet ministers, and many others who are in charge of appointing lower-level officials. In this way, the president may fill the government with people of the same political party. These officials then want to please the people who have the power to reappoint them.

President Leonel Fernández Reyna

Leonel Fernández Reyna was born in 1953 in Santo Domingo. Fernández spent much of his childhood in New York City. He returned to the Dominican Republic after high school and attended the University of Santo Domingo. In 1978, he earned a law degree, winning top honors.

Fernández helped found the Dominican Liberation Party (PLD) in 1973. The PLD focuses on helping poor and working people. Fernández advanced through the ranks of the party and, in 1996, at forty-two years old, became the youngest president in Dominican history. During his first term, the Dominican Republic became a popular tourist destination, and the nation's economy thrived. Fernández left office in 2000 but was elected president once again in 2004. Fernández is considered an innovative president, but many Dominicans are frustrated that he hasn't dealt with the problem of government corruption.

NATIONAL GOVERNMENT OF THE DOMINICAN REPUBLIC

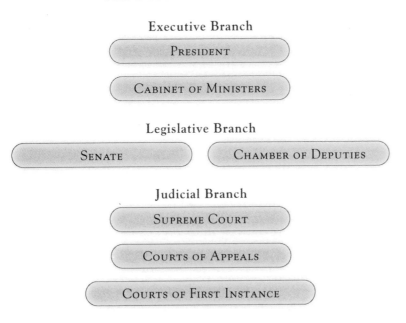

Executive Branch
PRESIDENT
CABINET OF MINISTERS

Legislative Branch
SENATE   CHAMBER OF DEPUTIES

Judicial Branch
SUPREME COURT
COURTS OF APPEALS
COURTS OF FIRST INSTANCE

The president is in charge of all diplomatic relations and can veto (cancel) bills passed by the congress. As commander of the armed forces, the president makes military appointments and decides when to send out troops. In a time of emergency, the president has the power to take over all branches of the government. During such times, all civil rights are suspended.

The Legislative Branch

The Senate and the Chamber of Deputies, together called the National Congress, form the legislative branch of government. The Senate has 32 members, and the Chamber of Deputies has about 150 members. All members of the legislative branch are elected by popular vote every four years.

Only the legislative branch has the power to declare a state of emergency. This helps prevent a president from misusing power and creating another dictatorship. The congress also gives the president an annual evaluation and approves or rejects the president's proposals.

The president leads the executive branch of the government. Here, a former president, Hipólito Mejía, addresses the members of the National Congress.

The Dominican Republic's court system forms the country's judicial branch of government. Most cases are heard in courts of first instance. If citizens think a court made a mistake, they can ask a court of appeals to review the decision. The highest court in the Dominican Republic is the Supreme Court. The Supreme Court reviews decisions made by appeals courts. It

The National Anthem

The Dominican national anthem, "Himno Nacional" ("National Anthem"), refers to the country as Quisqueya. This was the Taíno name for Hispaniola, and Dominicans use this as a nickname for their country. Emilio Prud'homme wrote the words to the national anthem, and José Réyes wrote the music.

Spanish lyrics

Quisqueyanos valientes, alcemos
Nuestro canto con viva emoción,
Y del mundo a la faz ostentemos
Nuestro invicto glorioso pendón.
¡Salve el pueblo que in trépido y fuerte,
A la guerra a morir se lanzó!
Cuando en bélico reto de muerte
Sus cadenas de esclavo rompió.

Ningun pueblo ser libre merece
Si es esclavo indolente y servil;
Si en su pecho la llama no crece
Que templó el heroismo viril.
Mas Quisqueya la indómita y brava
Siempre altiva la frente alzará:
Que si fuere mil veces esclava
Otras tantas ser libre sabrá.

English translation

Brave men of Quisqueya,
Let us sing with strong feeling
And let us show to the world
Our invincible, glorious banner.
Hail, O people who, strong and intrepid,
Launched into war and went to death!
Under a warlike menace of death,
You broke your chains of slavery.

No country deserves to be free
If it is an indolent and servile slave,
If the call does not grow loud within it,
Tempered by a virile heroism.
But the brave and indomitable Quisqueya
Will always hold its head high,
For if it were a thousand times enslaved,
It would a thousand times regain freedom.

also decides cases concerning the president and other government officials and cases concerning constitutional issues.

The Supreme Court has nine members, or justices. At the beginning of each presidential term, a group called the National Judiciary Council appoints members of the Supreme Court to four-year terms. The National Judiciary Council is made up of the president, members of congress, and two members of the Supreme Court.

The Supreme Court justices, in turn, appoint judges for all other levels of the court system, including in local governments. Because of this system of appointments, even local courts are tied to the president, undermining citizens' trust in the judicial system.

Former president Hipólito Mejía arrives in court to testify in a case.

The National Flag

The national flag of the Dominican Republic is red, white, and blue, with the Dominican coat of arms in the center. The blue sections of the flag represent liberty, while the red sections stand for the blood of the heroes who died to preserve it. The white area, in the shape of a cross dividing the red and blue, is a symbol of salvation.

The Dominican coat of arms shows a shield with a Bible and a cross. A ribbon above the shield reads *Dios, Patria, Libertad*, which means "God, Fatherland, Liberty."

Another ribbon below the shield reads *República Dominicana*, meaning "Dominican Republic."

People accused of crimes in the Dominican Republic are assumed to be guilty before their trial. Suspects can be held in jail for any length of time—sometimes even years—before having their day in court.

Local Government

The Dominican Republic is divided into thirty-one provinces and one national district, Santo Domingo (like the District of Columbia in the United States). Each has its own governor, whom the president appoints. Provinces are divided into municipalities, which are further broken down into townships. Local residents elect the councils of municipalities and towns.

Voting

All Dominicans aged eighteen and older can vote unless they are police, military, or prisoners. Although Dominicans have had the right to vote since 1942, the tradition of free elections is still new in the Dominican Republic. For many years, elections were suspected of being rigged and choices were limited. In recent decades, however, Dominicans have begun to hold elected officials accountable. Some Dominicans, especially those who remember the Trujillo era, still fear that ballots are not secret. They believe they might be punished if they do not vote as their employers or the government tells them.

Dominicans cast ballots in an election in 2006.

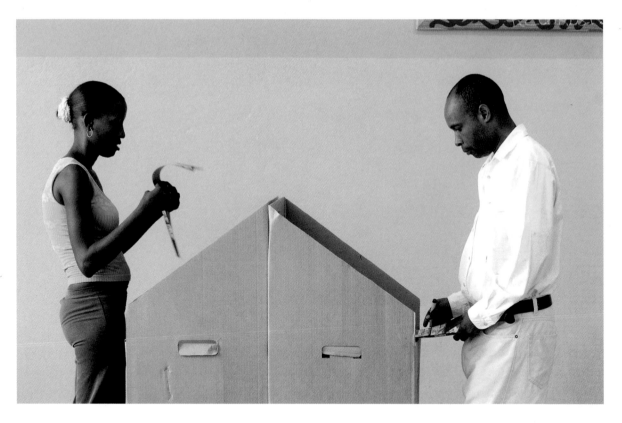

Santo Domingo: Did You Know This?

Santo Domingo sits at the mouth of the Ozama River, which empties into the Caribbean Sea on the southern coast. Its population of more than two million is rising rapidly. The city is home to many middle-class people. It is also home to a large number of poor people from rural areas who moved to the city to find work. This influx of people has led to housing and electricity shortages. Blackouts—periods when the electricity supply fails—are common.

Founded in 1498, Santo Domingo is the Western Hemisphere's oldest city built by Europeans. It proudly boasts the first university in the Americas, the University of Santo Domingo (founded in 1538), and the oldest church in the West Indies, the Cathedral of Santa María la Menor (completed in 1540).

Today, many of the city's historical sites and neighborhoods have been restored to allow visitors to experience its rich history. Las Casas Reales Museum has exhibits on Columbus's journeys and Spanish Caribbean history.

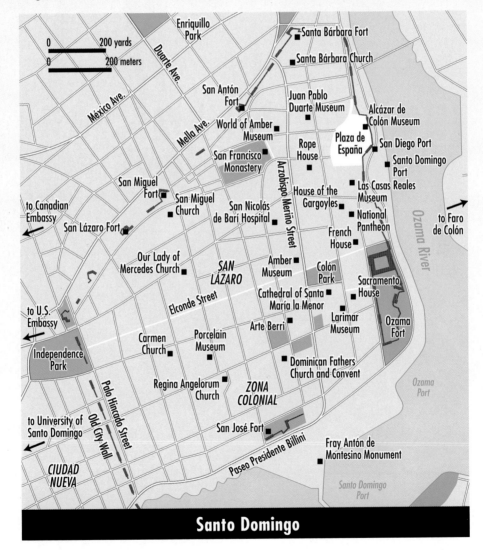

Santo Domingo

From Sugar
to Tourism

Many Dominicans depend on tourism for their living. Here, Dominican dancers welcome arriving tourists.

Traditionally, the Dominican economy was based on agriculture. Sugar was long the dominant industry. In recent years, tourism has become central to the economy, as visitors from all over the world arrive to enjoy the nation's sandy beaches and vibrant culture.

Agriculture

Agriculture now employs only 16 percent of the Dominican workforce. Many rural Dominicans have small plots of land, which the entire family works. They raise a variety of crops,

Opposite: **A Dominican farmworker clears a sugarcane field.**

Life in the Sugar Fields

Working conditions on the major sugar-cane farms are often dreadful. Most Dominicans won't work for the low wages paid for work in the cane fields. As a result, companies hire Haitians to work in the fields. The Haitians work as many as fifteen hours a day, and some are as young as eight years old. The Haitian workers are provided with shelter—tiny, crowded shacks called *bayetes* that have no running water, bathrooms, or cooking facilities.

such as rice and root vegetables, along with livestock, such as pigs, for meat; chickens, for eggs; and goats, for dairy products. It is a hard living. Many of these poor farmers, called *campesinos*, make crafts and other goods to sell to tourists in an attempt to make enough money to survive.

Large companies that grow cash crops own much of the farmland in the Dominican Republic. Altogether, nearly 600,000 acres (about 240,000 hectares) are devoted to growing sugarcane, mostly on the southern and eastern coasts. The State Sugar Council (CEA) is the largest sugarcane producer. It was established in 1966 when the government took over the large plantations owned by the Trujillo family.

Another profitable crop is tobacco, which people have grown on Hispaniola since the time of the Taínos. Dominican tobacco mostly is used to make cigars. The industry flourished in the 1970s, but the 1980s brought low prices and a number of devastating crop diseases. Tobacco farms recovered in the 1990s, and the export of Dominican cigars is now a key part of the economy.

The Dominican Republic also exports cocoa, coffee, ornamental plants, and winter vegetables. These are vegetables that people want to buy in the United States and Canada but that farmers cannot grow there during the cold winter months.

The country's fertile farmlands produce a wide variety of vegetables.

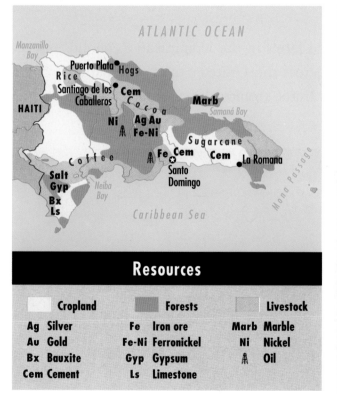

Resources

	Cropland		Forests		Livestock
Ag	Silver	Fe	Iron ore	Marb	Marble
Au	Gold	Fe-Ni	Ferronickel	Ni	Nickel
Bx	Bauxite	Gyp	Gypsum	⚒	Oil
Cem	Cement	Ls	Limestone		

Agriculture (2000)

Sugarcane	4,785,000 metric tons
Rice	527,000 metric tons
Cattle	1,900,000 head

Manufacturing

Cement (2001)	2,785,000 metric tons
Fuel oil (2002)	1,129,000 metric tons
Refined sugar (2002)	516,000 metric tons

Mining

Nickel (2002)	38,859 metric tons
Gold (1999)	651 kilograms

Thanks in part to farms in the Dominican Republic, grocery stores in cities across the United States and Canada offer a variety of citrus fruits, tropical fruits, and tender vegetables all year-round.

Cocoa beans grow in large pods on the cacao tree. The Dominican Republic is the world's eighth-largest cocoa bean producer.

Dominicans grow many other crops primarily for themselves and people visiting their nation. These include rice, beans, plantains, and cassava, a plant used for making tapioca, among other things. Corn, bananas, peanuts, tomatoes, lettuce, and cabbage are also staple crops. Fruits such as avocados, mangoes, guavas, passion fruit, tamarinds, and coconuts are grown year-round. People grow vegetables such as scallions, onions, and garlic in gardens all over the island.

In eastern sections of the country, more than 2.2 million beef cattle live on large ranches. Most of their meat is exported. Chickens and pigs are raised to be consumed by people in the Dominican Republic. Dominicans raise sheep for both meat and wool.

Millions of chickens are raised in the Dominican Republic. Most of them are consumed in the Dominican Republic rather than exported.

From the Fields to the Table

It takes many steps to turn the thick, tough stalks of sugarcane into fine, white crystals of refined sugar. After workers harvest the cane, the stalks are washed, shredded, and placed in a machine that sprays the strands of cane with water that dissolves the sugar. The resulting fluid is called cane juice.

This juice is heated, and lime is added to clear impurities. The solution is then infused with carbon dioxide to get rid of the extra lime. The liquid is poured into big tanks and heated until it thickens into syrup. This syrup is then transferred to large pans, where it is boiled until sugar crystals form. A machine spins the mixture so that all the crystals separate from one another. These crystals (right), called raw sugar, are tan.

To make pure white sugar, the raw sugar is rinsed and dissolved again. The solution is filtered many times until it is clear. Then, once again, it is heated into a syrup, crystallized, and separated. The result is refined white sugar.

Manufacturing

Sugar processing is a major industry in the Dominican Republic. The industry processes 1 million tons (910,000 metric tons) of sugarcane every year. Much of it is turned into refined white sugar. Sugarcane is also used to make molasses and rum. The Dominican Republic exports about three-quarters of its processed sugar to the United States.

The Dominican Republic also produces textiles, chemicals, fuel oil, medicines, and cement. Approximately 15 percent of the country's workers have jobs in manufacturing.

Most of the nation's industrial and manufacturing work occurs in free-trade zones. The zones are filled with foreign factories, usually belonging to American or Japanese companies. The Dominican government supplies the buildings, and the companies do not have to pay taxes on the raw materials they import. Labor is cheap, with plenty of people available for work. And the companies export the finished products at a discounted tax rate. All this means high profits for foreign companies. The goods made in free-trade zones account for about 70 percent of the nation's exports.

Most workers in free-trade-zone factories are Dominican women who accept very low wages from factory owners who know there is always another woman in search of a job. These workers sometimes put in as many as seventy-five hours a week at the factories. They often receive no health benefits, no vacation time, and no paid sick leave. Such factories are sometimes called sweatshops. As a result of public awareness and outcry, in recent years the government has set a minimum wage that foreign-owned companies must pay their workers.

Despite the problems with free-trade zones, they have boosted the economy in the Dominican Republic. Many factories purchase supplies and raw materials directly from Dominican companies, so they have become intertwined with the local economy. But the free-trade zones do not offer long-term economic security. The companies do not hesitate to move to other countries when they find a better deal.

Free-trade zones give tax breaks to foreign companies. This young Dominican worker stitches a shoe in a free-trade-zone factory.

The Dominican Republic has a long history of mining gold, silver, and nickel. Here, engineers meet in Los Cacaos at one of the Western Hemisphere's largest gold mines.

Mining

Since Europeans found gold in what is now the Dominican Republic five hundred years ago, mining has been important to the region. The earth still holds gold and silver, along with nickel, copper, iron, bauxite, and mercury. The nickel mines in the central part of the country produce about 33,000 tons (30,000 metric tons) each year.

Money Facts

The nation's official currency is the Dominican peso, which is divided into 100 centavos. Paper bills are available in values of 1,000, 500, 50, 20, 10, and 5 pesos. Coins come in denominations of 25, 10, 5, and 1 peso and 50, 25, 10, 5, and 1 centavo, although people no longer use centavos because inflation has made them worth practically nothing. In 2008, 1 Dominican peso equaled 3¢ and US$1 equaled 34 pesos.

The paper bills show images of significant political figures, such as Ramón Matías Mella and Juan Pablo Duarte, and landmarks such as the Cathedral of Santa María la Menor.

Open-air markets offer fresh produce. The women at this market in the town of Samaná are selling papayas and other fruits and vegetables.

Services

About 63 percent of working Dominicans have jobs in service industries. This includes people who work in many different fields, including banking, schools, restaurants, and tourism.

Though some upper- and middle-class Dominicans shop at modern supermarkets, most people go to the open-air markets or central market buildings, where farmers, butchers, fishmongers, and others bring their goods to sell directly to consumers. Here, vendors sell everything from fruits and vegetables to household items and clothing.

Striking a Bargain

Unlike in a store where prices are fixed, in a market, shoppers and sellers expect to haggle over the price. This tradition is full of quick exchanges of pretend disbelief. The vendor acts offended at the suggestion of a lower price, while the buyer claims that such a high price is ridiculous. Finally, the situation is resolved with a compromise, and everyone leaves confident that they have gotten the best of the bargain.

Beach-loving tourists bask in the sun on the country's northern coast.

Tourism

The Dominican Republic's sandy beaches and year-round sunny weather make it an ideal vacation spot. The nation earned an estimated US$3.5 billion in revenues from tourism in 2006, making it the country's largest industry.

The peak tourist season is mid-December through mid-April, reflecting the coldest seasons in Europe and North America, rather than the best seasons on the island. During the off-season, the number of tourists and the prices of tourist services drop dramatically. Much of the money tourists spend goes to foreign-owned resorts, but many visitors prefer to explore the countryside and Santo Domingo, contributing directly to the local economy.

Getting Around

The Dominican Republic is home to more than nine million people, but it has fewer than six hundred thousand passenger cars. So how do Dominicans get around? They rarely use trains, which are mostly used to transport freight. In fact, none of the nation's 321 miles (517 km) of railroad even enter Santo Domingo, and many of the railway lines do not connect to one another.

Instead, many Dominicans ride bicycles. Mopeds and motorcycles are popular among those who can afford them, especially in Santo Domingo, where riders can quickly (if dangerously) move through backed-up traffic and the old, nar-

A moped rider zips down a street in Santo Domingo.

row city streets. Privately owned taxicabs stop to pick up passengers beside the road. People pile in and on the vehicles, each paying a few pesos, until the cabs are overflowing. Passengers even sit on the fenders. These informal "buses" carry thousands of Dominicans each day. Larger cities and tourist areas offer more expensive taxis similar to those in the United States, Canada, and Europe.

La Gente

*L*A GENTE IS SPANISH FOR "the people," "the nation," or "the family." The multiple meanings of this term reflect the spirit of the people— one nation, one family.

In July 2006, an estimated 9,183,984 people made their homes in the Dominican Republic. About 59 percent of these people live in urban areas, while 41 percent lived in rural areas. If this seems like a fairly even distribution, consider that Santo Domingo and Santiago are the only major urban areas in the Dominican Republic. This means that more than half of the population is packed into two large cities and a few smaller ones.

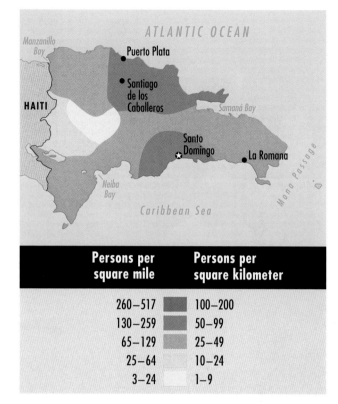

Persons per square mile		Persons per square kilometer
260–517		100–200
130–259		50–99
65–129		25–49
25–64		10–24
3–24		1–9

Dominican Society

The Dominican Republic has distinct social classes. The largest socioeconomic group is economically disadvantaged. About one-quarter of this group is unemployed. Typically, economically disadvantaged women are more likely to be employed than men in the same economic group. Many of these women work long hours to support their families. But most families in the lower class still don't make enough to meet their needs.

Opposite: A woman in Sosúa carries a bowl of fruit on her head.

Dominicans await an
Independence Day parade
in La Vega.

Population of Major Cities

Santo Domingo	2,412,000
Santiago de los Caballeros	690,548
Puerto Plata	255,061
La Romana	191,303

In rural areas, small landowners and migrant laborers struggle to make ends meet. Some move to the city for work and a chance for a more secure future. But affordable housing in cities is scarce, and some people live in run-down areas that lack basic necessities such as electricity and running water. Most people who move to the city keep ties with their rural relatives; they help each other in times of need. They call this tie a *cadena*, which means "chain."

There are approximately five hundred thousand Haitians in the Dominican Republic. Many work in sugarcane fields where the pay is low. In addition to the economic hardship, many Haitians in the Dominican Republic also face discrimination.

In recent years, a middle class has emerged in the Dominican Republic for the first time in its history. Today,

Ethnic Origins of Dominicans

Mixed	73%
European	16%
African	11%

These children of Haitian migrant workers attend a school at a Dominican sugar plantation.

about one-third of Dominicans consider themselves middle class. Many own shops or work in government. The middle class is extremely vulnerable to economic changes, especially in the sugar and tourism industries, which are the sources of much of their income. People in the middle class gain status and power through money, rather than through family or political ties.

For the first time in history, the Dominican Republic has a middle class.

In the Dominican Republic, the rich are called *la gente buena*, or *la gente culta*. This means "the good people" or "the refined people." Strong family ties have great influence on social standing.

A family enjoys a meal together.

Leaving Home

Because of limited opportunities at home, many Dominicans leave the country in search of a better way of life. Many who find jobs abroad send money back to support their families. New immigrants often already have family in the United States, easing the transition.

Dominican Americans celebrate their heritage at a Dominican Day parade in New York City.

Most Dominicans go to the United States, especially to New York City. Dominicans have been moving to New York in large numbers since the 1960s. They now make up the second-largest Latino group in New York City, trailing only Puerto Ricans. Each August, more than a half million people line the streets of New York for the Dominican Day parade. Other cities such as Passaic, New Jersey; Lawrence, Massachusetts; and Providence, Rhode Island, also have thriving Dominican communities. In some neighborhoods, Dominican restaurants and grocery stores line the streets.

Many Dominicans have found success in the United States. There, they have started their own businesses and become teachers and lawyers. And their children attend college at a high rate. At the same time, many Dominican immigrants miss the people and beaches and mountains that they left behind. Many long to return to their island home.

The Dominican Republic has a longstanding housing shortage. In the past, cities filled up with rural families looking for work, and streets and alleyways filled with makeshift shelters that had no drinking-water or sewage systems. Matters finally got so bad in 1995 that residents of the shantytowns filled the local churches and refused to leave until something was done. The government ignored their pleas and sent in troops to force residents back to their homes. The government promised new building projects, but instead tore down the shacks and erected monuments to attract tourists.

This section of Santo Domingo has no running water or sanitation. The houses are rundown and overcrowded.

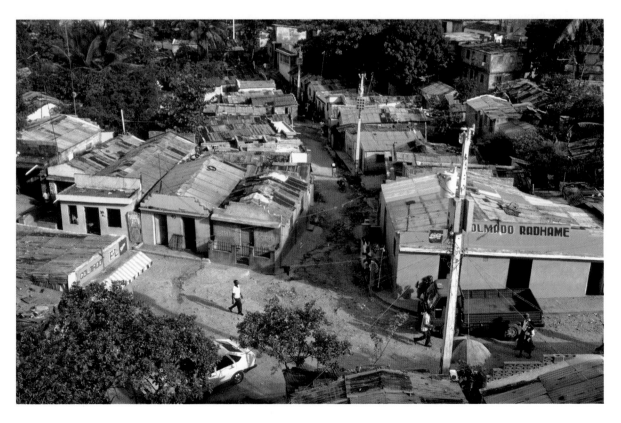

Blackout

The Dominican Republic does not have an adequate supply of electricity, and blackouts are common. The blackouts can last for a few hours or a few days. Either way, they cause many problems. Offices and factories shut down. Refrigerators don't work, so there is no way to keep food cold. Each year, parts of the Dominican Republic lose power for at least five hundred hours. That equals twenty full days and nights without electricity.

The situation has improved. By 2004, 95 percent of the population had clean drinking water (97 percent in urban areas, and 91 percent in rural areas). About 81 percent of urban families have adequate bathroom facilities in their homes.

The upper class in the Dominican Republic enjoy many of the same luxuries and activities as well-off people in the United States and Canada. This home was built for wealthy Dominicans.

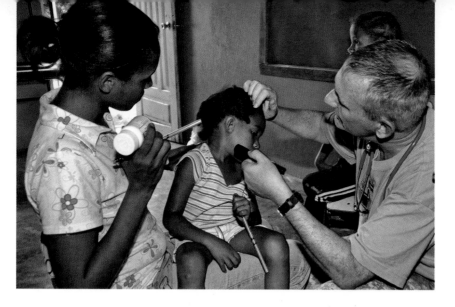

Most children in the Dominican Republic receive vaccinations at medical exams.

Health

The average Dominican man lives to be sixty-five years old, while the average woman can expect to live seventy-two years. By comparison, in the United States, the average life expectancy for men is seventy-five and for women is eighty-one.

In the Dominican Republic, there are fewer than two doctors for every one thousand people. Health care is poorly managed and far too expensive for most people. International efforts have ensured that most children receive vaccinations, protecting them from serious diseases. Nutrition is improving, but about 11 percent of Dominican babies are born underweight.

Education

All children in the Dominican Republic must attend school for seven years. In many places, however, schools are badly understaffed, and many do not offer all of the required grades. Owing to the cost of books and the need for extra family income, many economically disadvantaged children cannot attend school for more than a year or two. Many parents need their children to care for younger brothers and sisters while the parents are at work. Others need the children themselves to work to help the family survive. Still, many schools are successful, and the literacy rate—the percentage of people who can read and write—is high. About 87 percent of Dominicans are literate.

About 65 percent of Dominican children continue their education in secondary school, which lasts six years. There are now nearly a thousand secondary schools available to all children. Many economically advantaged children go to Europe or the United States for their secondary and university educations. Most Dominican universities are privately owned. The nation's only public university is the University of Santo Domingo.

In 2005, the Presidential Forum for Excellence in Dominican Education was created with goals to improve and expand schools for youngsters and to train adults in important careers such as information technology. Another goal of the program is to increase the number of years that children stay in school. Many private companies and organizations are helping by building schools in remote areas and funding teachers.

Dominican third graders work on their studies.

Most Dominicans speak and read Spanish.

A Land of Voices

The Spanish brought many things to Hispaniola, including a language. Spanish is the official language of the Dominican Republic. It has been enriched by various African and Taíno words.

The Spanish adopted some words from the Taíno language because Spanish had no word for a particular thing. Plants like tobacco (*tabaco*) and cassava (*casabe*) kept their native names, as did the hammock (*hamaca*), canoe (*canoa*), and hurricane (*huracán*).

African words such as *Vodou*, which is often called voodoo in the United States and is *vodú* in Spanish, arrived with enslaved workers and made their way into Spanish. The word for a hex or bad omen, *fucú*, came from an African language. To break this spell, you say *zafa*, another African word.

Common Spanish Words and Phrases

Sí	Yes
No	No
Bueno	Good
¿Cómo está usted?	How are you?
Por favor	Please
Gracias	Thank you
De nada	You're welcome
¿Qué hora es?	What time is it?
¿Habla inglés?	Do you speak English?
Hola	Hello
Adiós	Good-bye

Religious
Traditions

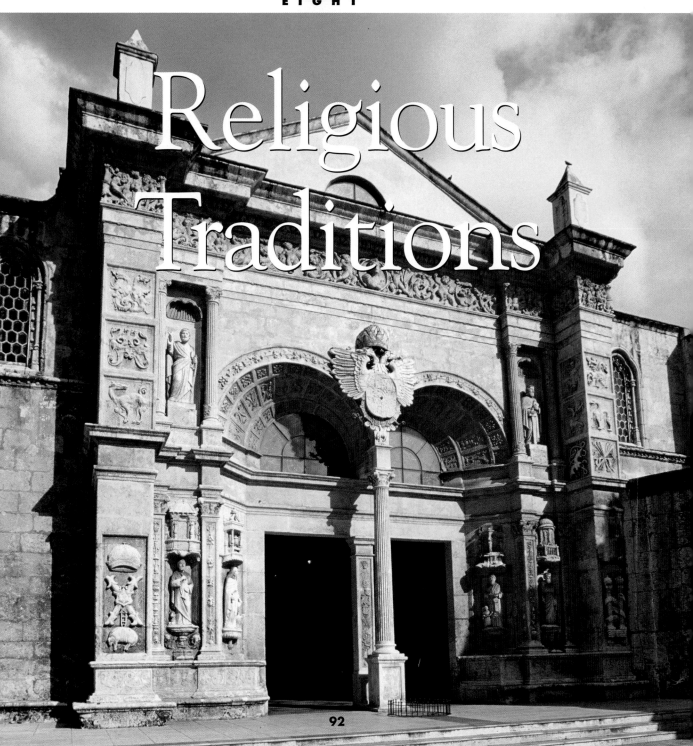

The Spanish brought Roman Catholicism to Hispaniola. This engraving shows a monk attempting to convert Hatuey, the leader of the Taíno resistance to the Spanish, before he is executed.

THE CONSTITUTION OF THE DOMINICAN REPUBLIC STATES that all citizens have freedom of religion. Most Dominicans are Roman Catholic, while some are Protestant or Jewish. Some people in the Dominican Republic also practice traditional religions, and a small number practice Vodou.

Roman Catholicism

About 95 percent of Dominicans are Roman Catholic. The Spanish brought Roman Catholicism when they arrived in Hispaniola. In 1494, Spanish priests held the first Catholic mass in the Americas near a settlement called Isabela, and in

Opposite: **Workers began building the Cathedral of Santa María la Menor in Santo Domingo in 1514. It was not completed until 1540.**

The Cathedral of Santa María la Menor in Santo Domingo is almost five hundred years old.

1540, the Cathedral of Santa María la Menor was completed in Santo Domingo. Six years later, the first archbishop of the island was named.

In colonial days, the Church was a major power in governing the island, but when the Spanish withdrew, the Church's importance fell dramatically. In 1954, Rafael Trujillo proclaimed Roman Catholicism the national religion and then used the Church to control the people. For the most part, Church officials overlooked the darker side of Trujillo's

When Pope John Paul II visited the Dominican Republic in 1992 to observe the five hundredth anniversary of Catholicism in the Americas, he celebrated mass at the Faro de Colón, an enormous monument the government built in Santo Domingo to honor Christopher Columbus. Entire neighborhoods of low-income houses were destroyed to make room for this massive monument in the shape of a cross. Many people thought that it was not right for the head of the Catholic Church to visit the monument, which resulted in the loss of so many homes. They refused to attend the mass. Despite the bad feelings, the government insisted that the mass be held there to highlight the monument.

politics. Finally, in 1960, religious leaders began to protest the arrests of those who opposed the dictator.

Priests are considered the most trusted of confidants, often serving not only as spiritual guides, but also as political and social leaders. Many work on economic issues, fighting to end poverty. And many nuns teach in schools or colleges, work as nurses, or run orphanages.

In the Dominican Republic, religion is sometimes very public. In rural areas, large processions called *rosarios* are held in hopes of curing an illness or solving problems such as drought or other natural disasters. The leader carries a large rosary (a set of prayer beads) and an image of the Virgin Mary

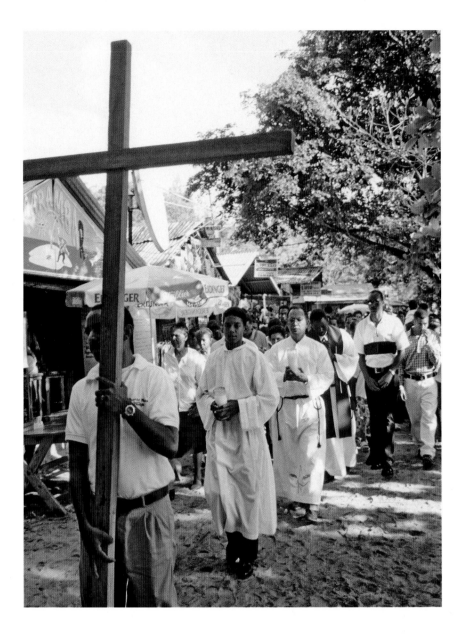

Religious processions are common in the Dominican Republic. This one is in Sosúa.

or another saint. Musicians follow behind the leader, playing guitars, flutes, and other instruments. At the rear of the procession are many people who follow along, singing and

Superstitions

Like people everywhere, some Dominicans are superstitious. Called *oraciones*, these "rules" tell people how to avoid bad luck and prevent unwanted ills. Here are a few:

- It is bad luck if a wedding guest wears black.
- If a couple is wed in November, the marriage will not last.
- Opening an umbrella in the house invites bad luck.
- If a person sleeps with his feet pointed toward the front of the house, he will die.

A statue of Saint Anthony towers near Santo Domingo Harbor. The statue is 150 feet (45 m) tall.

praying. It is believed that all of the members of the procession must stay with the group until the end for the prayers to be answered.

As the rosario passes from town to town, the group stops at stations, also called *rosarios*, which consist of groups of crosses erected as meeting places for the processions and as symbols of welcome to any traveler.

Religious sites and statues are important symbols of faith for many Catholic Dominicans. A statue of Saint Anthony located in Santo Domingo is considered a sacred shrine. It is said that removing the statue from its pedestal can cause earthquakes. The most important shrine on the island houses the painting *Nuestra Señora de la Altagracia* (*Our Lady of Altagracia*), an image of Mary, Jesus's mother. She is considered the island's protector. Many Dominicans travel to the shrine where the image is housed to pray.

Almost every Dominican home also has a shrine. In middle-class and wealthy homes, a statue of Mary or another saint may stand on a lace cloth, decorated with a bouquet of fresh flowers. In a tiny shack, a faded picture of a saint decorated with a wilted ribbon may serve as a shrine for its residents.

Many visitors come to this modern church in Higuey. It houses the painting *Nuestra Señora de la Altagracia* (*Our Lady of Altagracia*).

Some Dominicans visit brujos, or witch doctors, such as this man.

Spiritual Traditions

In rural areas of the Dominican Republic, believers often combine Roman Catholicism with other spiritual traditions. One of the most respected practices is that of the *ensalmo*. This is a healing chant, usually performed by an elderly woman. Healers, who can be either men or women, are called *curanderos*, and they work through saints, asking special help for those in need. Both men and women can also be *brujos*, or witch doctors. Brujos use herbs and other natural objects for healing. They are also believed to have the power to banish evil spirits.

This colorful Protestant church is located in the Samaná province.

Protestantism

About 2 percent of Dominicans are Protestant. Many of them belong to the Episcopal Church and the Dominican Evangelical Church. Others attend the Free Methodist Church, the Assemblies of God, and the Seventh-Day Adventists.

Many Dominican Protestants are the descendants of North Americans who brought their own faiths when they came to the island in the early 1800s.

A Town That Refugees Built

During World War II (1939–1945), Dominican president Rafael Trujillo invited Jews who were being persecuted in Europe to the Dominican Republic. He promised them land on the northern coast. A number of grateful refugees, most from Austria, settled there in 1939, establishing the town of Sosúa. They cleared the land and began dairy farms. To this day, some of their descendants live in Sosúa. A museum dedicated to the town's history sits on the main street along with a small synagogue. In 1991, some of the town's original settlers and their relatives came from all over the world to celebrate the founding of Sosúa.

Judaism

The Dominican Republic has a tiny Jewish population. A group of Jewish refugees built the small town of Sosúa on the northern coast during World War II. Today, Sosúa remains a center for the nation's Jewish population. Santo Domingo also has a synogogue, a Jewish house of worship.

Some European Jews escaped to the Dominican Republic during World War II. They built this synagogue in Sosúa.

Vodou

The rich mixture of the island has contributed to the religion called Vodou, which is found in different forms in several Caribbean countries. The Dominican form is called *Gaga*. It mixes African, Taíno, and Roman Catholic spiritual practices, with its strongest influence coming from the Dahomey region of Africa. The word *vodou* means "god," "spirit," or "sacred object." In the Vodou religion, there is one supreme being and many lesser spirits. Each individual has a protector spirit who rewards him or her with wealth and punishes with illness. Nature gods oversee the external world and are worshipped in seasonal celebrations. Family gods—the souls of dead ancestors—must be remembered with elaborate funerals and memorials so they will continue to protect the living.

Male Vodou priests are called *hungans*, while female priests are called *mambos*. As well as serving as spiritual guides, mambos and hungans are called on to rid

Dominicans take part in a Vodou ceremony.

the human body of *loas*, gods that possess the body. They also perform a ritual called *fa-a*, in which they scatter the kernels from palm trees on a cloth and then use the kernels' pattern to predict the future and solve problems.

Among Dominicans, those who live along the Haitian border are more likely to practice Vodou. Most practice their religion in secret. Although no religion is illegal in the Dominican Republic, people who don't practice Vodou tend to look down on those who do. Vodou products, however, can be found in markets throughout the Dominican Republic. This is probably more for the curiosity of tourists than for people practicing the religion.

Vodou potions and objects are sold in markets throughout the Dominican Republic.

CHAPTER

NINE

Arts and Sports

DOMINICANS HAVE LONG VALUED STORYTELLING. IN THE past, stories were passed from generation to generation, to entertain and instruct the young. The television set has interfered with this custom as many people, young and old, now sit and watch TV instead of talking. Some folk traditions have lived on, however. Many Dominican folk tales and fables began in Africa. One series of adventures involves Lapén, a cheeky rabbit who gets into scrapes, but escapes by using his wits.

Opposite: **These wood carvings are from the town of Sosúa.**

As in most countries, television is popular in the Dominican Republic.

Folk Arts

Handmade crafts, such as carved calabash gourds, are popular. People use the dried gourd to make ornate masks or containers. If the gourds are still filled with seeds, they can be made into rattling *maracas*, instruments used in merengue music. Many traditional crafts have survived, in part, because tourists like to buy locally made crafts as souvenirs.

Pottery figures for Christmas nativity scenes, which show the birth of Jesus, are another popular handmade craft. The figures are often made of unglazed terra-cotta, a type of clay. A nativity set may have seven or eight people and an array of animals that include sheep, cows, and burros. It is common for the figures of Joseph and the shepherds to wear large sombreros (hats).

Many rural women practice a craft called macramé, which involves knotting twine into elaborate bags, pocketbooks, and hammocks. Macramé can be done easily at home and requires little besides twine, so it costs the artist almost nothing but time. Macramé crafts are popular among tourists and provide income for the crafters.

Other traditional Dominican skills include woodcarving, palm-weaving, and making jewelry from corals and seashells. It is common to see young men selling colorful necklaces of shell beads along the beaches.

An Island Beat

Music is an ever-present part of Dominican life. On every street corner and from every storefront, music puts rhythm into the

Today's merengue bands feature more instruments than in the past. This band includes guitars and maracas.

steps of passersby. This is the land of *merengue*, a lively music with an African beat.

Originally, the merengue was performed using the *tambora* (a drum with two ends), the *güira* (scraper), and the accordion. Like most folk music, its sound has changed over the years. In the twentieth century, the saxophone was introduced, and now merengue bands include guitars, flutes, and maracas. The lyrics that accompany these traditional sounds can cover any topic, from love to politics. Every year, musicians from all over the Dominican Republic gather during the last week of July at a large merengue festival in Santo Domingo.

Music in the Dominican Republic is enriched by a wide variety of influences. As with merengue, African traditions contribute to the popular sound of reggae music. Spanish influences also bring the unmistakable Latin beat and the sounds of guitar to the island. Folk dances are still performed on special occasions to traditional music.

Dominican dancers perform wearing traditional dress.

Literature

For years, only members of the wealthiest Dominican families received a formal education, so they were the only Dominicans who could enjoy literature. As with other forms of Dominican culture, literary works and styles from other parts of the world have heavily influenced Dominican literature. Besides Spanish influences, Dominican writers took inspiration from work produced in France and other European countries.

Most Dominican literature has reflected the world's artistic trends. The strongest movement in the early twentieth century was modernism, led by Gastón Fernando Deligne. He

Politics and Literature

Two presidents of the Dominican Republic have contributed to the island's literature. Juan Bosch Gaviño (left), considered one of the three greatest Dominican writers, wrote many short stories about his time spent in exile. His political rival, Joaquín Balaguer Ricardo, who served as president for twenty-eight years, was a poet.

Julia Álvarez began her career as a poet. She has written novels, essays, and children's books.

wrote dark, personal poems. Another Dominican poet, Pedro Mir, wrote poems about the social conditions of the time. Mir was forced to leave the Dominican Republic for much of the Trujillo dictatorship.

Many more recent authors have spent at least part of their lives in the United States, and this shows in their writing. Julia Álvarez was born in New York. Her family returned to the Dominican Republic when she was an infant. When she was ten years old, her family's efforts opposing the Trujillo regime were discovered, and they fled back to New York. Álvarez writes about the immigrant experience and living between two cultures in such books as *How the García Girls Lost Their Accents*. Junot Díaz is another writer who delves into the struggles of adapting to life in the United States. In 2007, he won the Sargeant First Novel Prize for *The Brief and Wondrous Life of Oscar Wao*.

Dominicans play a pickup baseball game in the Cordillera Central.

In 1891, the Dominican Republic's Cuban neighbors introduced a sport that would become a way of life in the country. U.S. troops had brought baseball to Cuba. Early on, Dominican plantation owners encouraged people to play the sport as a way of keeping workers occupied during slow seasons. In the 1920s, baseball leagues began in the Dominican Republic. Today, baseball is the most popular Dominican sport.

The best Dominican players compete in the Dominican Baseball League. Each year, Major League teams from the United States send recruiters to the Dominican Republic to sign contracts with the best young players. More than one hundred Dominicans play in baseball's Major Leagues today. Top Dominican players include home-run hero David "Big Papi" Ortiz, pitcher Pedro Martínez, slugger Manny Ramirez, and all-star first baseman Albert Pujols. Dominican baseball players on North American teams are considered heroes back home for more than their sports achievements. Many Dominican players regularly donate money and resources to their communities, never forgetting where they came from.

The Major League Baseball association, the player's union, and several private companies have started a program called the Baseball Tomorrow Fund. Money from this fund has built baseball fields and bought equipment for boys and girls in areas in the Dominican Republic. This program aims to build leadership skills and self esteem through sports. Other national programs combine baseball programs with educational advances while encouraging children to become more involved in their communities.

Some of the world's best baseball players come from the Dominican Republic. Here, Dominican Anderson Hernández hits the ball during a game in Santo Domingo.

Island Life

Dominicans place great value on family and friendship.

Dominicans generally face life with optimism and good spirits. Despite a variety of challenges, the people try to make the best of what they have. Whether living in the peaceful country or the busy city, all Dominicans brave life with the help of friends and family.

Women and Men

Traditionally, men and women in the Dominican Republic followed strict gender roles. Men were seen as protectors, while women were supposed to be mild-mannered, quiet, and helpful. But these attitudes are changing.

Opposite: **Dominicans make the most of their island life.**

This young woman studies a plant sample as part of her job as a laboratory technician in the town of Jarabacoa. Professional opportunities for women in the Dominican Republic are growing.

In recent years, women have made great strides. President Joaquín Balaguer Ricardo appointed several women to important state offices such as provincial governor. They are beginning to have more social and political influence.

Saying Hello

How people say hello depends on their gender and how well they know each other. Younger Dominicans greet each other by clasping hands, much like a handshake in the United States and Canada. Most men greet each other with a handshake, although close friends may hug. When a man and a woman meet, a swift kiss on the cheek is also common. When a woman greets a woman, a kiss on the cheek is the usual greeting. Most of these customs are rooted in Spanish traditions.

What's Your Name?

In the United States and Canada, it is common for parents to give a child one or two first, or given, names followed by the surname (the last, or family, name) of the father. In this way, names trace a person's lineage, or family history, primarily through the father's side of the family. In the Dominican Republic, the system is more complicated.

Take, for example, a man named Carlos Santiago Fonseca. Carlos is his given name. His father's surname, Santiago, is the name that will be passed on to his children, while Fonseca is his mother's surname. He has a daughter named María, so her childhood name is María Santiago. When María grows up, she marries a man named Eduardo Martín Núñez. Her married name is María Santiago de Martín. Two years later, she has a son. He is named José, so his full name becomes José Martín Santiago. When María has a daughter, Esperanza, the child's name is simply Esperanza Martín, until she is married.

Marriage

In the Dominican Republic, people can choose between a religious wedding and a civil service. More than 80 percent decide on a civil marriage, called a free union, because it is much less expensive.

A Dominican bride has photos taken before her wedding.

Island Life **117**

Middle- and upper-class people usually have a church wedding. Afterward, friends and family gather for a large, elaborate party.

Family

The bond within families in the Dominican Republic is strong. Many people trust only family. Family members are responsible for helping in time of sickness and financial need. The family unit extends to include *compadres*, or godparents.

Godparents are considered essential to a child's upbringing. Once a close family friend becomes a godparent, his or

Nearly one in three Domincians is less than fifteen years old.

A Dominican family prays at the table before eating.

her relationship with the parents changes from friendship to something more formal. Godparents help pay for events such as baptisms, marriages, and funerals. They are also expected to help pay for a child's medical care and education. The godparent is a protective figure who usually spoils the child; children, in turn, treat godparents with a great deal of love and respect.

Death in the Family

When a family member becomes seriously ill, relatives, friends, and neighbors gather at the house and help the family care for the sick person. If the person dies, the whole family comes and stays until the next day for the funeral. For the nine days following death, called la novena, only the back door of the house may be used. La novena is a time of mourning. It is filled with tears, wailing, and song. People pray for the dead person's soul, and family members talk constantly of his or her virtues. On the one-year anniversary of a death, the family gathers to mourn and remember their loved one.

This typical house in the mountains of the Samaná province is painted in bright colors.

Home, Sweet Home

For most rural people in the Dominican Republic, home is a simple building made of whatever materials are available. Most live in *bohíos*, huts built with bamboo and palm leaves. Sometimes, rural Dominicans add mud, plaster, stones, and reeds to make the house sturdier. The most basic homes have dirt floors, while those belonging to people with a little more money have cement floors. Tin or zinc roofs are also considered a sign of wealth. Homes are often painted in bright colors.

Some villages, especially in the mountains, include houses made of wood. These have one main room and a separate cookhouse so that the main room will not get too hot or fill with smoke during meal preparation. Towns usually cluster around a church and one or two tiny stores, each with a window that serves as a counter. A slightly larger town may also have a butcher shop and a small store or pool hall.

Dominican suburbs are now filling with middle-class houses, which are similar to small suburban homes in U.S. or Canadian cities. The wealthy of the city live apart, in homes surrounded by high walls and gates.

In Santo Domingo, riverside shacks lie just across the street from comfortable housing.

Dominican Holidays

New Year's Day	January 1
Epiphany (Three Kings Day)	January 6
Our Lady of Altagracia Day	January 21
Juan Pablo Duarte's Birthday	January 26
Independence Day	February 27
Good Friday	March or April (date varies)
Easter	March or April (date varies)
Labor Day	May 1
Corpus Christi	June 17
Restoration Day	August 16
Our Lady of Mercedes Day	September 24
Constitution Day	November 10
Christmas	December 25

Relaxing

After a long day of work, most Dominicans spend their time relaxing with friends. In small towns, groups gather at the local store or restaurant and pass the evening talking. Sundays are the main day of relaxation, when families gather in the center of town for conversation and games. As the women and children return home to prepare the evening meal, men stay behind to watch a baseball game. Many times, families will gather on the streets to play neighborhood games of baseball.

In more urban areas, groups of young people might go out together. In general, the wealthier the family, the more likely

Dominicans relax with a game of dominoes.

their child, especially a girl, will have a chaperone. If a young couple is dating, they will often join other couples in groups to go out.

Dominican folk dancers entertain at a restaurant in Santo Domingo.

Many Dominicans enjoy an active nightlife. In the cities, Dominicans dress in their best clothes and go to clubs and restaurants, which nearly always have music for dancing. For those who cannot afford expensive places, the sidewalk becomes the dance floor. Musicians play on the streets, and the long stretch of Santo Domingo's waterfront becomes an outdoor party. In the villages, the single road through town may become the dance floor, with a group of local people playing instruments or a radio filling the night air with music. Cars weave their way carefully between the dancers to get through town.

Wearing devilish masks and colorful costumes, revelers dance during the Carnival parade of Santo Domingo.

The Dominican Way of Celebrating

Festivals are a big part of Dominican life. One of the best-known and biggest festivals is Carnival, which is a last celebration before Lent, the somber period leading up to Easter. The nation's major Carnival festival is in Santo Domingo, where a big parade winds through the streets.

In preparation for the parade, everyone makes elaborate costumes and builds and decorates huge floats. The most popular costume is a *diablo cojuelo*, a devilish creature with the power to rid the body of evil. Children make masks portraying this devil, who has huge horns and teeth. Other traditional masks look like animals or are decorated with jewels.

As the procession moves through the street, it passes rows of vendors who play loud merengue music and sell food and souvenirs late into the night. The parade includes a group of whirling women called *marimantas*. They wear long white dresses with wide skirts that swirl around them as they dance. Near them dance *la muerte enjipe*, a group of men wearing black suits painted with skeletons. The carnival festivities continue for two days and right through the night.

Glorious Food

Dominican food is varied and hearty. Plantains are an essential part of the Dominican diet. Although plantains look like large bananas, they have thicker skins and are not as sweet. People cook plantains before they eat them. Sometimes people slice them thin and fry them like potato chips, but more

Conch fritters are deep fried pieces of battered shellfish.

often, they make fried plantain patties, called *tostones*. Root vegetables, such as sweet potatoes, taro, and yams, are also common foods in the Dominican Republic.

Typical meats include goat and pork, as well as chicken. Along the coast, many people enjoy seafood, making meals of fish such as cod, salmon, shark, and tuna. The most popular shellfish is conch, which is often made into fritters. Dominicans like to use coconut to sweeten seafood dishes. Beans are important to the Dominican diet and an excellent source of protein. *Sancocho*, a stew made with chicken, cassava, plantains, and spices, is a popular, hearty dish.

Breakfast and lunch are the most important meals of the day for Dominicans, especially in rural areas. Breakfast often has to carry a worker through a long morning of labor in the fields, so it may be heavy in starches such as plantains. Breakfast sometimes includes a boiled root vegetable.

Lunch is the biggest meal of the day. Dominicans eat lunch right before the afternoon rest, or *siesta*. Lunch can include almost anything. Rice and beans is traditional, or rice and beans served with chicken, fish, or meat.

Dinner, which people eat late in the evening, usually consists of breads and vegetables. Eggs are also common in the evening meal. Fried dumplings filled with meat or cheese, called *quipes*, are a popular dinner meal. Some people enjoy

Mangú

Mangú, a puree of green plantains, is a traditional breakfast food. It provides Dominican workers and schoolchildren with a good start for their day.

Ingredients
1 large green plantain

$\frac{1}{2}$ tsp. salt

$\frac{1}{2}$ onion, sliced

2 tbsp. cooking oil

Directions
1. Wash the plantain well and boil it for 20 minutes. Cooking time may vary depending on the size of the plantain, but it must be soft enough to mash after it is peeled.

2. Let it cool and then remove and discard the skin. Place the plantain in a bowl, adding the salt and $\frac{1}{3}$

cup of the liquid the plantain was boiled in. Mash well.

3. Put the plantain in a blender or food processor and puree.

4. Sauté the onions in the oil.

5. Serve the plantains in a bowl with the onion spread over the top.

Flan is a favorite Dominican dessert. This flan is made with mango and served with papaya.

a soup called *mondongo*, which is made from tripe, a cow's stomach. A cake called *pastelón* is baked with vegetables for added nutrition. Desserts are often very sweet. Popular desserts include corn pudding, candied sweet potatoes, and the Spanish caramel custard called *flan*.

On special occasions, such as Christmas or Easter, families sit together for large feasts. Roasted pig is a special meal for Christmas, usually served with pigeon peas (small, pale yellow beans) and other traditional dishes, such as boiled chestnuts. Fish is the traditional dish for Easter.

The Dominican national dish is a combination of stewed meat, rice, and beans. It is nicknamed *la bandera*, "the flag," because the white rice and red beans remind people of the colors of the Dominican flag. Dominicans eat it on Independence Day, as they recall their nation's long struggle for freedom.

Timeline

Dominican Republic History		World History	
People first settle the island of Hispaniola.	4000–3000 B.C.		
		2500 B.C.	Egyptians build the pyramids and the Sphinx in Giza.
		563 B.C.	The Buddha is born in India.
Arawaks begin arriving on Hispaniola from South America.	ca. A.D. 300		
		A.D. 313	The Roman emperor Constantine legalizes Christianity.
		610	The Prophet Muhammad begins preaching a new religion called Islam.
		1054	The Eastern (Orthodox) and Western (Roman Catholic) Churches break apart.
		1095	The Crusades begin.
		1215	King John seals the Magna Carta.
		1300s	The Renaissance begins in Italy.
		1347	The plague sweeps through Europe.
		1453	Ottoman Turks capture Constantinople, conquering the Byzantine Empire.
Christopher Columbus lands on Hispaniola.	1492	1492	Columbus arrives in North America.
Isabela, the first permanent European settlement on Hispaniola, is founded.	1493		
The Taíno culture is almost entirely extinct.	1524	1500s	Reformers break away from the Catholic Church, and Protestantism is born.
Some pirates make Hispaniola their base.	1600s–1700s		
Under the Treaty of Ryswick, Hispaniola is divided between Spain and France.	1697		
		1776	The U.S. Declaration of Independence is signed.
		1789	The French Revolution begins.

Dominican Republic History

Haiti takes over Spanish Hispaniola.	**1822**
Dominicans declare independence on February 27.	**1844**
Dominican leader Pedro Santana invites Spain to retake the Dominican Republic.	**1861**
Spain's control of the Dominican Republic ends.	**1865**
The Dominican Republic falls deeply into debt.	**1880s**
The United States takes control of Dominican customs houses.	**1905**
The United States occupies the Dominican Republic.	**1916–1924**
Rafael Trujillo rules the Dominican Republic as a dictator.	**1930–1961**
Trujillo is assassinated on May 30.	**1961**
Dominicans hold their first free elections since 1924.	**1962**
The United States intervenes in a Dominican civil war.	**1965**
Crop diseases devastate the tobacco industry.	**1980s**
Leonel Fernández Reyna of the Dominican Liberation Party (PLD) is elected president.	**1996**
Hurricane Georges hits the Dominican Republic, causing damage costing an estimated US$6 billion.	**1998**
The Dominican Republic suffers an ecnomic crisis.	**Early 2000s**
Leonel Fernández Reyna is reelected.	**2004**

World History

1865	The American Civil War ends.
1879	The first practical light bulb is invented.
1914	World War I begins.
1917	The Bolshevik Revolution brings communism to Russia.
1929	A worldwide economic depression begins.
1939	World War II begins.
1945	World War II ends.
1957	The Vietnam War begins.
1969	Humans land on the moon.
1975	The Vietnam War ends.
1989	The Berlin Wall is torn down as communism crumbles in Eastern Europe.
1991	The Soviet Union breaks into separate countries.
2001	Terrorists attack the World Trade Center in New York City and the Pentagon in Arlington, Virginia.

Fast Facts

Official name: República Dominicana (Dominican Republic)

Capital: Santo Domingo

Official language: Spanish

Santo Domingo

DOMINICAN REPUBLIC

- • Cities of more than 100,000 people
- ○ Other cities
- ⊙ National capital

0   50 miles

0   50 kilometers

ATLANTIC OCEAN

Manzanillo Bay

Monte Cristi

Puerto Plata

Sosúa

Yaque del Norte R.

Santiago de los Caballeros

Nagua

Santa Bárbara de Samaná

Dajabón

Mao

La Vega

San Francisco de Macoris

Samaná Bay

HAITI

José Armando Bermúdez National Park

Los Haitises National Park

Miches

José del Carmen Ramírez Nat'l Park

Bonao

Hato Mayor

Las Matas de Farfán

Yaque del Sur R.

San Juan de la Maguana

Ozama R.

Monte Plata

San Pedro de Macoris

Higüey

Neiba

San Cristóbal

La Romana

Duvergé

Azua

Santo Domingo

Barahona

Neiba Bay

Baní

Soona Island

Mona Passage

Pedernales

Enriquillo

Oviedo

Beata Island

Caribbean Sea

Dominican Republic

Dominican Republic's flag

Fish in coastal waters

Year of founding:	1844
Founder:	Juan Pablo Duarte
National anthem:	"Himno Nacional" ("National Anthem")
Type of government:	Republic
Chief of state:	President
Head of government:	President
Area:	18,816 square miles (48,734 sq km)
Greatest distance east to west:	240 miles (385 km)
Greatest distance north to south:	170 miles (275 km)
Length of coastline:	800 miles (1,300 km)
Bordering country:	Haiti
Highest elevation:	Pico Duarte, 10,417 feet (3,175 km)
Lowest elevation:	Lago Enriqillo, 150 feet (46 m) below sea level
Average temperatures:	July, 81°F (27°C); January, 75°F (24°C)
Average annual rainfall:	In the mountains, 100 inches (250 cm); in the valleys, 50 inches (130 cm)
National population (2006 est.):	9,183,984

Cathedral of Santa María
la Menor

Currency

Population of largest cities:

Santo Domingo	2,412,000
Santiago de los Caballeros	690,548
Puerto Plata	255,061
La Romana	191,303

Famous landmarks:
- ▶ *Alcázar*, Santo Domingo
- ▶ *Cathedral of Santa María la Menor*, Santo Domingo
- ▶ *Faro de Colón*, Santo Domingo
- ▶ *Las Casas Reales Museum*, Santo Domingo
- ▶ *Lago Enriquillo*, La Descubierta

Industry: The Dominican Republic's two most profitable industries are sugar processing and tourism. Sugarcane is the nation's most profitable crop. Tourism accounts for about half the nation's yearly income. It replaced sugar as the nation's largest industry in 1984.

Currency: The Dominican peso; in 2008, 1 peso equaled 3¢, and US$1 equaled 34 pesos.

System of weights and measures: Officially, the Dominican Republic uses the metric system, but U.S. measures such as pounds, miles, and gallons are also common.

Literacy rate: 87%

Web Sites

▶ **Dominican Republic Embassy Kid's Page**
www.domrep.org/kids.html
For information about Dominican history, music, and food.

▶ **DominicanRepublic.com**
www.dominicanrepublic.com
To learn more about the nation's culture and economy.

▶ **The World Factbook: Dominican Republic**
https://www.cia.gov/library/publications/the-world-factbook/geos/dr.html
For lots of quick facts about the Dominican people, government, and economy.

Organizations and Embassies

▶ **Embassy of the Dominican Republic**
1715 22nd St., NW
Washington, DC 20008
202-332-6280
www.domrep.org

▶ **Embassy of the Dominican Republic in Canada**
130 Albert St.
Ottawa, Ontario
K1P 5G4
613-569-9893
www.drembassy.org/english/

Index

Page numbers in *italics* indicate illustrations.

Photo Credits

age fotostock: 109 (Juan Bellapart), 14, 15, 77, 120 (Gardel Bertrand), 70 (Heeb Christian), 56 (Dave Collins), 122 (Sylvain Grandadam), 72 (Kevin O'Hara)

Alamy Images: 31 top (blickwinkel), 114 (Ian Dagnall), 33 (Reinhard Dirscherl), 7 bottom, 80 (ImageState), 99 (Mike Long), 29 (John Mitchell), 41 (M. Timothy O'Keefe), 125 (Shane Pinder), 96 (Nicholas Pitt), 103, 123 (James Quine)

Animals Animals/Breck P. Kent: 20

AP Images: 63, 76 top, 111, 133 bottom (Ramon Espinosa), 124 (Andres Leighton), 101 (John Riley), 52

Art Directors and TRIP Photo Library: 104, 118 (Helene Rogers), 91 (Bob Turner)

Art Resource, NY: 11 (Albert Bierstadt/ The Newark Museum), 93 (Bildarchiv Preussischer Kulturbesitz)

Bridgeman Art Library International Ltd., London/New York: 42 (Samuel Lane/ The Crown Estate), 43 bottom (Private Collection)

Corbis Images: 73 (Tony Arruza), 90, 57, 65, 113 (Orlando Barria/epa), 18 top (Tom Bean), 44, 46, 48, 49, 53, 54, 110 right (Bettmann), 55 (C. Douce & E. Alonso), 110 left (Hulton-Deutsch Collection), 13 (Catherine Karnow), 83, 133 top (Gideon Mendel), 74 (Ryman/photocuisine), 88 (Tim Street-Porter/Beateworks)

Danita Delimont Stock Photography/Greg Johnston: 35 bottom

Digital Railroad: 17 (Tom Bean), 97 (M. Timothy O'Keefe), 59, 94, 132 top (Tom & Therisa Stack/Tom Stack & Associates), 117 (Stephan Zaubitzer)

Getty Images: 119 (Matt Henry Gunther), 51 (Thomas D. McAvoy), 61 (Omar Torres)

Landov, LLC: 21 (Kena Betancur/Reuters), 58 (Eduardo Munoz/Reuters), 60 (Eric Thayer/Reuters)

MapQuest.com, Inc.: 64, 131 top

Masterfile: 68 (Janet Bailey), 2, 69

North Wind Picture Archives: 12

Panos Pictures: 115 (Jean-Leo Dugast), 25 (Sean Sprague), 87 (Philip Wolmuth)

Peter Arnold Inc./Achim Pohl: 75, 102

Photo Researchers, NY: 86 (David Grossman), 30 (Nicholas Smythe)

Photolibrary: 98 (Fred Derwal), 100 (Bertrand Gardel)

Photoshot/World Pictures: 23 left

Retna Ltd./Edwin Garcia: 76 bottom, 132 bottom

Reuters/Str Old: 105

StockFood, Inc./Caspar Carlott: 127

Superstock, Inc.: cover, back cover, 6, 34 (age fotostock), 92 (Angelo Cavalli), 85 (Hola), 47 (Image Asset Management Ltd.), 32, 131 bottom (Prisma), 36

The Granger Collection, New York/KPA/ ullstein bild: 18 bottom

The Image Works: 107 (Mario Algaze), 78 (Jan Becker/Visum), 22 (Kike Calvo/ VW), 79 (Stuart Cohen), 31 bottom (Townsend P. Dickinson), 40 (Mary Evans Picture Library), 89 (Photri/Topham), 45 (Print Collector/HIP), 116 (Sean Sprague), 121 (Topham/Pressnet)

TIPS Images: 66, 130 left

Tom Bean: 7 top, 19, 23 right, 26, 27, 28, 38, 71 right, 82, 84, 95, 112

VIREO/Academy of Natural Sciences of Philadelphia/C. Nadeau: 35 top

Woodfin Camp & Associates: 8, 9, 24 (Michael Friedel), 108 (Catherine Karnow).

Maps by XNR Productions, Inc.

Studies, in the Area Handbook series, published by the Library of Congress. For current statistics, they looked to the World Health Organization, UNESCO, the Dominican Embassy, *The World Almanac and Book of Facts 2007*, and the *Encyclopedia Britannica 2007*'s online edition. To get a more personal view of the country, Lura interviewed people who have emigrated from the Dominican Republic to the United States.

Barbara studied history and English at Boston University, and Lura majored in English at Skidmore College. They have written a number of travel guides, along with books for young people about Peru, South Africa, and Zambia. They worked together on *Frommer's America on Wheels: New York and New England*. Lura wrote about New Hampshire and Vermont, while Barbara wrote driving tours for each. Barbara has written guides to the Galapagos Islands, Portugal, eastern Canada and New England, and together Barbara and Lura spent several months traveling in Europe while researching *Exploring Europe by Boat*. Lura and Barbara both live in New Hampshire.

Photo Credits

Meet the Authors

Lura Rogers (far right) and Barbara Radcliffe Rogers, a daughter-mother team, first became interested in the Dominican Republic when they visited the Caribbean together on a cruise. They have since traveled and sailed in the Dominican Republic, renting a cottage in Sosúa overlooking Puerto Plata Bay.

During their stay in the Dominican Republic, Lura and Barbara became fascinated by Sosúa's unusual history. They learned the town's story from the owner of the cottage they rented. He was among a group of Jewish Austrians who fled Europe to escape persecution during World War II and settled in Sosúa, where they carved farms out of the forest. Interviewing the man from Sosúa made them eager to talk to other Dominicans to learn more about the country.

Both Lura and Barbara speak Spanish and enjoy practicing it when they travel. They also enjoy cooking. After they returned home, they made Dominican dishes, experimenting with substitute ingredients for those they could not find in the United States.

For reliable information on Dominican history and government, the authors used *Dominican Republic and Haiti: Country*